OpenSource

Astrophotography

2.2

*Your first low cost astro
photo from your backyard*

For my wife Dagmar, who had to give up a lot of our spare time for this book.

Content

Preface

Astrophotography is a great hobby, but it is generally considered to be difficult, expensive and time consuming. In this book I describe my way to overcome these problems.

The benefit of open source software is not only the reduction of the financial burden. It also facilitates the implementation of the hobby by a variety of software tools that are easy to install and a useful remedy for the problems in astrophotography. I use UBUNTU Linux and all the examples in this book use the software on this operating system. The software is platform independent (except fotoxx) and runs as well on Windows or Mac.

The focus of the hardware, which is described in this book, is also located in the low-cost area. A digital SLR or a mirrorless system camera is enough to start with. Important is the option of interchangeable lenses, especially that of a T2 adapter. No further adaptation is needed. The camera is mounted on the focuser of the telescope using the T2 adapter. In case you don't have a system camera with interchangeable lenses, a normal digital camera will do. In this case you might want to use a "digital mount", which holds the camera in front of the eyepiece.

Which telescope you want to use depends on your wallet. For getting started in astrophotography, you can safely use an inexpensive achromatic refractor telescope. If necessary this can be later used as a guide scope.

The telescope with a camera must finally be fixed on on a tripod or better on an equatorial mount. At this point, it becomes expensive: Even beginners should prefer a stable equatorial mount before a cheap "wobble mount". If you give up the hobby, a GOTO mount is easily sold on eBay.

After this introduction, I hope you will enjoy reading the book, have a lot of success with the implementation of the content and a lot of satisfaction when looking at the results.

One note to my language skills: This book is the translation of my German language book "OpenSource Astrophotografie 2.0". I apologize for any translation errors.

Karl Sarnow
December 2012

In the meantime, the German language version made an upgrade to version 2.2, motivated by the inclusion of more OpenSource software:

• The **INDI**-Interface for connecting a mount with a computer.

• The **gphoto2**-software to control your DSLR by your computer.

• The **darktable**-software, basing upon gphoto2.

• The **RawTherapee**-software, which allows the development of images from the camera sensors raw image.

This version of the eBook brings the upgrade to the English language version.
Karl Sarnow
July 2013

Legal remarks and warnings

Actuality of links

In the sources and links part of the book you will find many links to topics, I discuss in my book. As the Internet is fast changing, I cannot make sure, that the content you find at these links right now are still those, when I wrote the book. Although the links where created with great care, I cannot take any responsibility for the content of the links.

OpenSource license

Another issue is the license of use for OpenSource software. This kind of software is made available on an "as is" base. Which means, you can install and use the software without any cost, but also without any warranty. Nobody will guarantee the functionality or look of the software. Both might vary on different computers, different operating systems or different versions of the same software. Even different versions of the same operating system might influence look or functionality. The software authors even refuse any responsibility for any possible damages, the use of the software might cause. Be aware of that, before you install any OpenSource software and read the license conditions before you install the software.

Warning! Sun!

Each telescope has a manual in which the manufacturer warns not to look directly into the sun. This warning is also printed directly on the telescope. And obviously I expect that you follow the advice of the manufacturer of your equipment. Nevertheless I add this warning to my book, because it is really dangerous to look into the sun. Therefore here again the warning:

Never directly look into the sun or take photos of it

The sun is too bright and will cause blindness if you do not follow the warning.

General remarks

The author of this book writes about his personal experience and opinion. Not more, not less. Take this book as a suggestion, not an instruction. Always have in mind, that the suggestions of this book might not be applicable in your special situation. The handbook of your software and hardware is the definitive guide, which you have to follow, while my book is a collection of my experience with my software and hardware. In short: Do not try to use a part described in my book, when it does not fit into your camera system. Sometimes parts fit together mechanically, but the optical path lengths do not fit, ending up in an unsharp or even no image. The theory of the book is in this case not wrong. You have simply chosen optically not matching parts. Contact an experienced dealer for the actual selection of components to buy for your system.

Principles of
Astrophotography

Spaceship earth is your location

First of all: The earth is the spaceship in which we move through space and shoot images from our astronomical companions. This has consequences: Unlike in photography, astrophotographers have no firm stand on which you can mount your camera, because the earth rotates once every 24 hours around its polar axis. And any mount on earth follows with the same speed. The movement is visible with the naked eye. We might want to keep the movement as startrails perhaps later in an aesthetically pleasing image.

But as you know, through a telescope every movement seems faster. Thats why telescopes at tourist viewpoints are on tripods. Looking through such a sturdy tripod at the night sky, you can see the stars move at a constant speed through the field of view.

So if we want to take pictures of the night sky with a telescope, we have to move the telescope at the rotational velocity of the earth in the opposite direction. Then we make up for the rotation of the earth and the starry sky seems to be stopped in the telescope. Now we can also shoot the stars with long exposure times. We therefore want to get a telescope, which controls this reverse rotation with the help of a motor (figure 1).

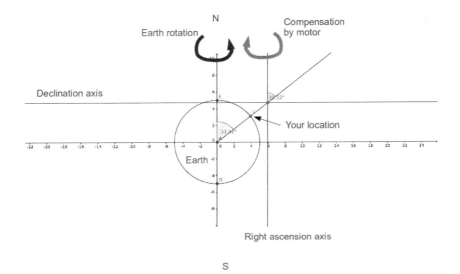

Figure 1: Compensation of earth rotation by motor in an equatorial telescope mount.

You will recognize, that the earth's rotation is compensated by a rotation around an axis parallel to the North-South axis. This parallel to the north-south axis in the telescope mount is called the right ascension axis (also called polar axis). If the motor is turned on, it follows the visible star in the telescope. The angle in the center of the earth is the latitude. It is 0 ° on the equator and +90 ° at the north pole. At the south pole the latitude is -90 °. When properly aligned, the right ascension axis must show the same angle at the mount as the local latitude. Figure 2 shows a simple equatorial mount.

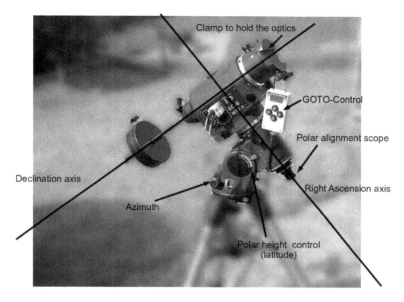

Figure 2: An equatorial telescope mount.

To set up the mount, it is rotated on the tripod in the azimuth right-left, until the polar alignment scope points toward Polaris (figure 3). Then move the mount up-down using the polar height control until Polaris is in the marking of the polar alignment scope.

To select any star, the telescope must be rotated around a second axis. This axis is perpendicular to the right ascension and is called the declination axis (figure 2). The rotation angle of right ascension and declination defines the location of an astronomical object (star, galaxy, ...). They are its coordinates. Unfortunately, however, the mount rotates continuously around the right ascension axis. Therefore, it was agreed that the the right ascension angle starts a certain point in the sky, the vernal equinox. Once the telescope points at this point, the angle of right ascension is 0h. It is actually measured in hours and not as usual in degrees.

Sky coordinates

The star Alcor, for example, the little horseman above the big wagon has the coordinates RA = 13h25m22s and DEC = 54 ° 55m28s. How can we find the star with an equatorial mount?

- Setup the mount and align the right ascension axis parallel to the earth.
- Align the telescope to the vernal equinox.
- Turn to the right ascension for 13h25m22s.
- Turn the declination for 54 ° 55m28s.

The star is in the eyepiece of the telescope. Quite simple isn't it? There still remain some simple questions.

- How will I know that the right ascension axis is aligned parallel to the axis of the earth?
- How do I find the vernal equinox?
- How can the right ascension set to 13h25m22s, while the right ascension axis is constantly rotating?

For the alignment of the right ascension axis (first question), there is a simple tool, the polar alignment finder. The mount is first aligned roughly north. You will find the letter N somewhere on the mount to help rough alignment. Through the hollow right ascension axis, a small telescope with a marker, the polar alignment scope, looks into the sky. By random, there is a star located close to the celestial north pole, called Polaris (figure 3). The telescope is now aligned by rotating the azimuth (right-left) and of latitude (up-down) so that Polaris is in the marking of the polar alignment scope (figure 4). As this procedure is quite easy, make sure your mount has a polar alignment scope built in.

Figure 3: Polaris is found near the North Celestial Pole.

The second and third questions cannot be answered that simple. The easiest way is to engage colleague computer. However the computer will help only, if it is built in the mount and if it controls the declination and right ascension axis. Then the mount is advertised as equatorial GOTO-mount. If reading the right ascension is a problem for you, the equatorial GOTO-mount is the solution for you. Once you have aligned the mount using the polar alignment scope as described, switch on the computer in the mount. The computer asks for a known visible star. After verification, you move the mount with the arrow keys on the remote control panel to the specified star and confirm on the control panel. That's it. Now you only need to enter the desired object. The telescope moves thanks to the GOTO control to the object in the telescope and the object should be visible in the middle of the eyepiece. More or less. So if the location of an object using the right ascension is a problem for you, you should insist on a GOTO mount. In this book, I assume that you have followed my advice and I will limit myself to the description of the use of a GOTO mount, if that should be necessary at all.

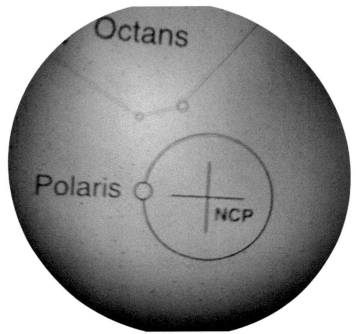

Figure 4: A view through the polar alignment scope.

The super-stable tripod

A properly aligned equatorial mount is now actually something like the tripod for astrophotographers. With careful alignment, exposure times of up to one minute without tracking control are possible. But good astrophotography occasionally requires exposure times of hours. So what to do then? In this case helps a second telescope, the guide scope, which is mounted parallel to the photographing scope. A digital camera at the back of the guide scope photographs continuously a star. Whenever the star moves in the guide scope, the digital camera sends a signal to the equatorial mount and brings it back on track. This procedure is called autoguiding and makes a GOTO mount a super stable mount, which allows exposure times of almost any length.

Proposals for the beginner

There are equatorial GOTO mounts available in the price range from € 500 to € 10,000. My experience is based on the HEQ5 and EQ6 mounts from Skywatcher, a low-cost Chinese manufacturer. Alternatively, the Celestron CAMGoto, Skywatcher EQ3Skyscan or Orion SkyView Pro Equatorial GoTo Telescope Mount, just to name 3 versions, are examples of other cheap equatorial GOTO mounts. They all have a clamp for the GP scope base. Most telescopes come with such a dovetail plate and can be mounted directly to the clamp. If you want to use astrophotography, avoid GOTO mounts that are not an equatorial mount. Most of these are less suitable for photography and use a fork mount or one arm mount. Check with your dealer. For visual observations, however these mounts are unmatched practical and handy.

The equipment needed

The mount

The mount is that part of the telescope, which carries the optics. It guarantees a centered object throughout the exposure time. Additionally, the mount (or better the built in computer) should allow fast finding of objects. And last not least, the mount must be stable enough to carry the optics with camera. Rugged and stable enough not start swinging in the wind. Below the mount is a tripod or column, holding contact to the earth. Normally both parts come together. As mentioned in the chapter *Principles of astrophotography* you should buy or own an equatorial GOTO mount.

The optics

The actual telescope optics consists of either a lens telescope (refractor) or a mirror telescope (reflector). If you want to start from scratch with the hobby, a combination of equatorial GOTO mount and optics is a good tip. If necessary, you can later exchange the optics. For starters, it should be a design with not too long focal length. A large aperture is of course good, because short exposure times are possible. But large aperture optics are expensive. For the beginner, the following chart may be helpful (table 1).

Type	Achromatic lens (Refractor, lens telescope)	Apochromatic lens (Refractor, lens scope)	Newton scope (Reflector, mirror scope)	Maksutov-Cassegrain scope (Mirror scope with lenses)	Schmidt-Cassegrain scope (Mirror scope with lenses)
Advantage	Low cost.	Good imaging quality. Large aperture.	Good imaging quality. Large aperture. Low cost.	Good image quality. Low cost. Long focal length. Reduced maintenance efforts.	Good imaging quality. Long focal length. Low maintenance efforts.
Disadvantage	Chromatic aberration, low aperture.	Expensive, Heavy.	Heavy, high level of maintenance.	Small aperture, long focal length.	Small aperture, long focal length.
Price range	200-500€	400-5000€	100-5000€	300-1000€	500-7000€
Remark	Low cost lens telescope. Less recommendable for ambitious amateurs. Well usable for hobby entrance.	Recommendable for ambitious amateurs. Focus length below 1000mm. Best for wide field photos.	Recommendable for ambitious amateurs. All focal lengths and apertures available. Requires more rugged mounts, due to the size of the scope. The mirrors must be adjusted frequently. Less for beginners.	Small aperture and long focal length require long exposure times. Therefore a better mount is recommended. For more experienced amateurs.	Like Maksutov-Cassegrain. Very good image quality, more for the ambitious amateur.

Table 1: Overview on scope types.

The beginner telescope for astrophotographers should be easy to transport, so you're ready to image quickly. Thus a combination of a small GOTO mount with a small refractor is suitable for "tasting blood". With about 700 € you are ready to go. But if you are not sure, a step by step introduction is given in the chapter "The first observation night".

The camera

The most important criterion of a camera for astrophotography is its sensitivity to light. However, we are not talking about special cameras for astrophotography. Those can easily reach the price range of € 10,000. No, let's go with a simple digital camera that we already own. If you think astrophotography is fun, you can still purchase a special astro camera.

Once you look at the digital camera market, you can distinguish the following types of digital cameras:

- Digital SLR. This type has an optical viewfinder through the lens. Maybe this seems a bit outdated, but it is not. No other viewfinder will allow you to see things in darkness like an optical viewfinder. Unique features are the interchangeable lenses that are mounted to the camera by a bayonet. Newer members of this category have a "live view" setting. If this feature is turned on, the mirror pops up and opens the optical pathway to the image sensor. The image can then be observed directly on the camera screen. This option is best suited to adjust the focus of the telescope.
- Digital system camera. This is on one hand the development of the digital SLR camera without a mirror, on the other hand a return to the good old Ur-Leica, and other representatives of cameras with interchangeable lens, but without a mirror for the TTL viewfinder. These cameras also have a bayonet mount for interchangeable lenses, yet without the mirror, and a "Live View" mode viewfinder only. For astrophotography this means, that you will not see objects except bright stars. Nevertheless, this is what you need for focusing.
- Digital camera with fixed lens. The traditional digital camera that can be used for afocal photography and Star Trails.

Particularly suitable because of the interchangeable lenses are only the SLR (optimally with Live View mode) and the system cameras. You can start with the normal digital camera, but very quickly feel the desire for a better solution.

In each case, the camera should allow manual adjustment of exposure, sensitivity and, in the case of a digital camera with fixed lens, a manual focus adjustment.

The camera's ISO sensitivity is one of the most important features. Here, however, considerable skepticism is recommended. It is important that the camera at high sensitivity is not too noisy. If you plan your next camera buy, read the test reports carefully. They normally do report about the behaviour at higher ISO settings.
In my case, I shoot with 6400ISO sensitivity and get quite usable shots (see below). Therefore, I recommend in any case a camera with at least 6400ISO sensitivity to look for. Table 2 below shows a selection of cameras with high maximum sensitivity.

Camera (Selection)	Maximal ISO-Sensitivity	Price (2012 in Europe)
Nikon D4	204800	from 5700 €
Canon EOS 6D	102400	from 2000 €
Pentax K5	51200	from 1000 €
Canon EOS 650D	25600	from 600 €
Nikon D5100	25600	from 450 €
Olympus E-PL5	25600	from 700 €
Sony NEX-5	25600	from 500 €
Panasonic LUMIX GH2	12800	from 800 €
Samsung NX1000	12800	from 450 €

Table 2: A selection of available cameras.

Focal astrophotography

You need a camera with an interchangeable lens. Either a system camera or a digital SLR. As the sensitivity is high enough, you may have such short exposure times that you can take photos of astronomical objects without autoguiding. This simplifies the start with astrophotography. Later you can still upgrade to guided astrophotography. But first you have to have a first success. You will need a T2 adapter for your camera. Once the world was taking photos with analog SLR cameras, there was a trick to connect all brands of lenses to cameras of nearly all manufacturers of the world. The trick: The lens had a T2 thread. And for each camera, there was a T2 adapter that fitted to the camera. The lens is then screwed into the T2 adapter and works fine on each camera to which a T2 adapter existed. And that was virtually any camera on the market. Astrophotographers today adapted that trick. There are eyepiece tubes with T2 thread that fit into the eyepiece holder of the telescope. At the end of the eyepiece tube, the T2 adapter of the camera takes the digital SLR or system camera. Now the camera and the telescope are a photographic unit. The image sensor of the camera is located in the focal plane of the telescope. (figure 5). This is the technique of professional astrophotographers and we make it ours.

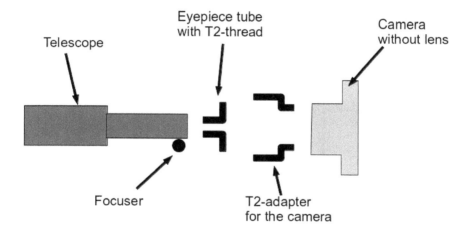

Figure 5: Adapting a camera with interchangeable lens to the telescope by a T2-adapter.

As said in the beginning, we restrict ourselves to amateur astrophotography cameras that are already present in the household of the reader. It should not be a secret that professional astrophotography is done only with special cooled image sensors. But this is a different league. Even DSLR or system cameras might not be available in your household so far. Nevertheless you can start with a standard digital camera, if you are not too ambitious with the selection of your objects.

Afocal eye piece projection

For this technique, a classic digital camera of each quality category will be enough. Helpful would be a manual focusing. It sets the focus to infinity. Such a prepared camera is fixed to the eyepiece with an eyepiece camera mount (figure 6).

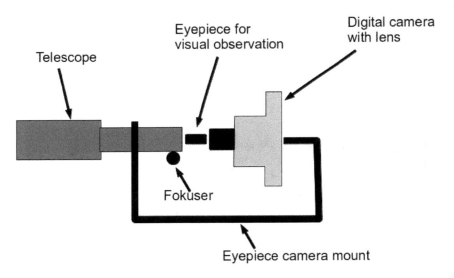

Figure 6: A standard digital camera is fixed to the eyepiece with an eyepiece camera mount.

Focusing is done with the focuser of the telescope, the lens of the camera remains set to infinity.

There are also special photo eyepieces available where the eyepiece itself has a T2-thread to directly connect to the lens of the camera. If the camera lens has a filter thread, as cameras had in analog times, there are adapter rings available that connect the eyepiece with T2-thread directly to the filter threads of the camera lens. Unfortunately, modern digital cameras do not have filter threads any more.

Focal eye piece projection

In this variant, a photo eyepiece with T2-thread is used to directly project the image of the astronomical object onto the image sensor of the camera. The advantage is to increase the focal length of the telescope. Unfortunately this also requires a camera with a removable lens (figure 7).

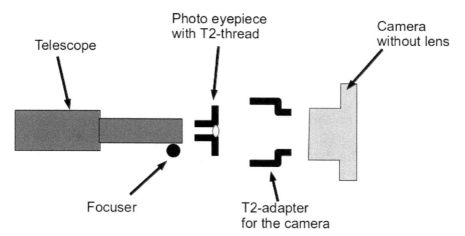

Figure 7: Using focal eye piece projection, the enlarged image on the image sensor is created by the eyepiece.

Astrophotography without a telescope

Of course you can take astrophotos directly with the built in lens. For this purpose, you should consider two arrangements:

- Photography with a photo tripod. The camera is not moved by a motor. The stars are therefore not shown as dots but draw a circular line around polaris.
- Mounting the camera with lens on the equatorial mount. There are GP-rails with a screw thread for connecting the camera. Then, the camera can be tracked with its own lens. Depending on the quality of the lens and the camera, you can have pretty wide field images.

In both cases, the focus of the lens should be set manually to infinity. If your camera does not have a manual focus setting, it will probably fail taking astronomical images by one of these two methods.

The shooting

Depending on the chosen method, the focus is set by the telescope focuser or the built in lens. The focus is controlled either directly on the display of the camera or a digital SLR optical viewfinder. If the digital SLR has a Live View mode, you should use it for focusing, but you will be limited to bright stars. So first align your camera to a bright star and then focus it. Do not change this focus setting while moving to other objects. For re-focusing, you have to move again to a bright star, because live view viewfinders are not able to detect low intensity astronomical objects.

If your camera allows you to manually set the shutter speed, set the longest possible exposure time (before the B setting, B for bulb). Allow up to 30 seconds at the maximum sensitivity of the camera (e.g. 6400ISO) for impressive pictures of the night sky. And always take more than one photo from the same object. I do always take 10 images for later adding of images with the GIMP.

My own technical equipment

Maybe it is interesting for beginners, with what equipment I'm currently taking my photos. Therefore, I have compiled table 3. My equipment is not professional and is based on my tight budget. Moreover, for me the quick setup and portability is important. Sure the equipment is not sufficient to fill a glossy book on astrophotography with superb Hubble quality images. But most of my friends are impressed by the quality achieved. Examples of photos made with this equipment can be found in [2]. Actually it turns out that careful alignment of the mount and taking advantage of the highest sensitivity level of new camera models with the longest exposure time of less than B (30s on the Nikon, Olympus in the 60s), the images from all telescopes show round stars, the criterion for no movement while the shutter was open. If the stars are not round, some shift occurred with open shutter.

Device	Price (ca. 9/2012 in Germany)	Features
Skywatcher HEQ5 Pro Synscan equatorial GOTO mount	944 €	Very transportable, easy to align, easy to operate equatorial GOTO mount.
ETX90 Maksutov-Cassegrain Telescope f=1250mm, d=90mm	829 €	Very small, very light, excellent image quality. Built in flip mirror to switch between visual observation and photography. My version is a bit older and has no GOTO part. The mentioned price is with GOTO fork mount. I removed the old (non-GOTO) fork mount and put the telescope tube on a GP dove tail plate. There are in the meanwhile similar telescopes from Asian manufacturers for less price, once you do not need the GOTO fork mount.

Device	Price (ca. 9/2012 in Germany)	Features
Orion ED80 achromatic refractor f=400mm, d=80mm	119 €	Small achromatic corrected lens scope with acceptable image quality. Originally intended to be used as a guide scope. But as it has a built in T2-thread, it is also very useful for wide field images.
Astro Professiona l ED102 Refraktor f=714mm, d=102mm	850 €	Larger apochromatic corrected lens scope with good image quality.
GSO newton type mirror scope f=800mm, d=200mm	478 €	Very bright photographic newton mirror telescope. Must be adjusted once before every observation night. A 2" coma corrector should be used to protect the image sensor and avoid coma in the photo. Very heavy weight and therefore less transportable.

Device	Price (ca. 9/2012 in Germany)	Features
Camera Olympus E-410.	n.a.	This older DSLR camera has a FourThirds mount (FT). It is no longer available. Successors are system cameras with the MicroFourThirds mount (MFT). The small image sensor size (half of 35mm film size negatives), triggers an effective doubling of the focal length of the telescope. With ISO1600 much less sensitive than my NIKON D5100 DSLR. This camera was one of the first ones with Live View mode.
Camera Nikon D5100	500 €	DSLR-Camera with up to 25600ISO sensitivity. The turnable monitor allows together with the Live View mode simple focusing without turning the neck. All photos I made with this camera were taken with 6400ISO and 30s exposure time at all telescopes without guiding.

Table 3: My personal equipment.

OpenSource Software for Astrophotography

There are three useful species of software for astrophotography:
1. Software for the preparation of the observation night.
2. Software for processing the results of the observation night.
3. Software for controlling the camera and/or the scope.

The first type of software helps you to select the objects to be observed and supports the alignment of the mount. The tools are called Kstars [5] and Stellarium [6].

Kstars is a cross-platform software for the display of the night sky in the form of maps. Anywhere in the world at any time. On the Kstars maps you can find 100 million stars, 13.000 deep sky objects, all 8 planets, the Sun and Moon, and thousands of comets and asteroids.

Stellarium has similar features, but the Stellarium screen tries to show you the sky in a photo realistic way. That is, at daylight you do not see stars but the sun and (sometimes) the moon. At twilight time, some zones of the screen are light, others are already dark and the brightest stars appear. Later on, the sky is shown as if you are in a desert. Nevertheless, in any case dew and atmospheric influence is visible. You can even display the landscape in the area, showing visibility restriction by surrounding trees and buildings. There is even a manual how to bring in your actual observation space into the Stellarium night.

The result of a well prepared observation night should be a set of astronomical photos. But these are not that brilliant as you can find them in glossy books about astronomy. They are in urgent need of refurbishment with a suitable image processing software, software of type 2. GIMP [4] is the tool of choice for this task. And once you are finished with GIMP, you might in some cases consider Fotoxx [16] for the final touch of HDR (High Dynamic Range) or stacked image processing. Unfortunately Fotoxx is so far only available for the LINUX operating system, although it is OpenSource. So maybe the program's source code is just waiting for you to translate it to windows or mac machines. In the section about more advanced techniques you find also RawTherapee [17], which develops photos in the RAW-format of your camera into JPG or TIF photos, which then are treated like the JPG photos you obtain normally from your camera.

A bit more experience requires the software of type 3: The INDI [18] (Instrument Neutral Distributed Interface) drivers allow you to control your scopes mount within Kstars and Stellarium, i.e. by a mouse click. You have to understand how to setup an RS-232 link from your computer to the mount and how to integrate the link into the programs Kstars or Stellarium (whichever you prefer).
Also a bit tricky is the use of gphoto2 [19], which is a terminal program to control a DSLR/system camera. May be you prefer to control the camera in a fine looking GUI program? Then darktable [20] is the program of choice, nevertheless just using gphoto2.
As these pieces of software are more for specialists, the description of it follows in a separate section about advanced techniques.

Kstars

At this point, I will describe how Kstars is used to prepare the observing night. The first step is telling Kstars where you are located. This is done through the menu "*Settings | Geographic*". This opens a menu with local proposals (figure 8). In the simplest case, choose a city nearby.

Figure 8: The geographic selection windows of Kstars.

The first step to observation is the installation of the telescope. For this purpose, the mount has to be aligned with the polar scope. With this scope you locate Polaris, the north star. But unfortunately Polaris is not exactly located on the skies north pole (NCP: North Celestial Pole). Like all stars it rotates around the nearby NCP. Kstars shows you where Polaris is located exactly at the specified time (figure 3). If you rotate the polar finder scope around the right ascension axis as Kstars shows Polaris, the mount is aligned quite accurately. However it should be noted that the polar finder scope is a simple Kepler type telescope. This means that the view is an image reversed view. So you should arrange the polar finder scope as indicated in figure 9: A thought red line goes through Polaris in Kstars, the NCP in Kstars, the NCP in the polar finder scope and Polaris in the polar finder scope.

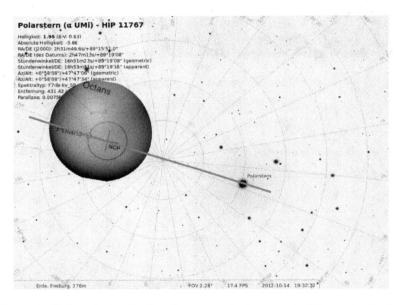

Figure 9: Kstars helps finding the correct alignment of the polar finder scope.

Then bring Polaris into the polar finder scopes marking by moving the azimuth angle (right-left) and the altitude angle (up-down).

The next steps in using the equatorial mount is the alignment to the spring equinox. Using a GOTO mount you simply have to select a bright star from a list, which you can clearly identify in the sky. Stellarium is better for this purpose, because the photo-realistic rendering supports the novice in the selection of a brilliant reference star. But Kstars also helps finding a suitable reference star.

To find the most suitable reference star for the calibration, the simple sky view is sufficient. It depends on the direction in which you have a clear view at the observation night (figure 10).

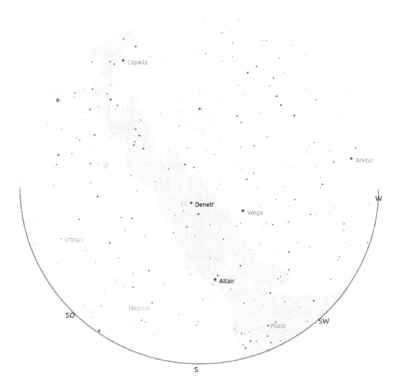

Figure 10: In the sky view you can choose the brightest stars as reference stars for the alignment of the mount (Inverse display).

If bright stars are seen, whose name is not listed, you can activate the context menu with a right click of the mouse and select the "Add label" entry.

In the above case, I would have chosen the Altair as a reference star because it was clearly visible in the southern sky.

We are now ready for the first observation. Once found, select it in the GOTO control. The telescope turns to the position where it assumes the star. You then have to move the scope using the GOTO control until the selected star is visible in the center of the eyepiece. Calibration done!

Now you can choose any object from the database of the GOTO control unit. Kstars can help you finding an interesting object in the dialog "*Tools | What's Up Tonight*" (figure 11).

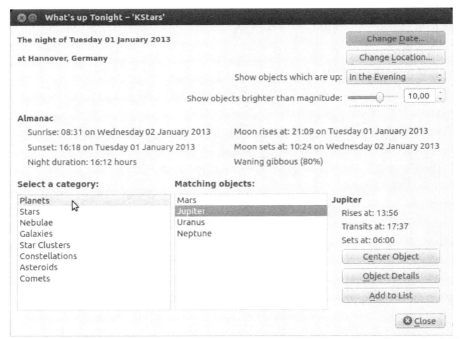

Figure 11: The dialogue presents the visible objects at the selected location.

This will be described in detail in the chapter "*The first observation night*".

Stellarium

Stellarium particularly impresses by its aesthetics. Stellarium therefore is the program more likely to be used. Also in the choice of reference stars, the photo-realistic rendering of the sky is useful.

The selection of the reference star is indeed most impressive. The corresponding sky view figure 12 shows a bright star in the southern sky (Altair). By clicking on it (circle) its data is shown in the upper left corner.

Figure 12: Stellarium shows the photo realistic night sky (Inverted display).

Again, in the section "*The first observation night*" I will explain how to use Stellarium for planning the observation at night.

GIMP

GIMP [4] is used after the results of the observation night are on the hard disk. The following tasks are done with GIMP:

- Most astrophotos are affected with artifacts that need to be removed. The most important task is to remove the lightning of the night sky in a city.
- The low brightness of astronomical objects requires the summation of many underexposed shots into a good exposed one.
- With long exposure times the image sensors noise increases. This noise is shown in a grainy structure, which can be removed by softening the image and/or averaging many noisy images into one without noise.
- By changing the brightness curve, fine image details can be worked out.

All this I will discuss in detail in the chapter "*After taking photos*".

Fotoxx

Fotoxx [16] is a combination of photographic archive and image editing software. For astronomy use, its capability to handle image clusters like HDR and image stacking is most important. This includes everything that has been listed under GIMP already. Fotoxx can not do anything what GIMP could not do as well. But especially for the creation of HDR (High Dynamic Range) images, Fotoxx is particularly easy to operate. Likewise, the image noise reduction by stacking of 2-9 images is easy. It is very easy to combine images by stacking and painting. Fotoxx starts operation after the images have been treated by GIMP. As I wrote before:

All this I will discuss in detail in the chapter "*After taking photos*".

RawTherapee

Once you own a DSLR or system camera, you will have noticed, that your camera enables you to save photos on the cameras memory chip in the RAW format. While saving a photo on the memory chip in a JPG format requires a tremendous computer program within the camera, running on the original bits of the camera sensor, the RAW image just saves a copy of the sensor chip's information. The disadvantage of the RAW type image is, that normal computers and displays cannot show it. The advantage is, that no preprocessing destroyed any information, hidden in details of the sensor chip. For example: A good cameras sensor chip saves the image in 14 bit per color pixel (or even more), while the JPG image only has 8 bit per color pixel. This means that each color pixel in the ready to view JPG image has 2^8=256 intensity levels, while in the original sensor pixel you find 2^{14}=16384 intensity levels. Much, much finer! This is where RawTherapee comes in: It allows you to stretch out the significant part of the astro image, before squeezing the sensor data into the 8 bit per color pixel corset of the JPG photo.

All this I will discuss in detail in the chapter "*After taking photos*".

The first observation night

Here we are: By way of exception a clear sky announces a good observation night early in the evening (Yes, I am living in a rainy part of the world). Now you should plan your short observation night. It follows a discussion of "how to" with Kstars and Stellarium. Then choose your favorite and try it yourself.

In the afternoon with Kstars

Date, time and location are set in Kstars using the menu entry "*Time | Set Time*" and "*Settings | Geographic*". Usually you will not take photos from a mountain but from your garden, which is surrounded by trees and buildings. So it's good to know beforehand which items you do not need to look for.

For the beginner, star clusters are the most rewarding objects, followed by galaxies and nebulae. Planets require a large focal length of the telescope. Less than one meter focal length is not promising for a planets photo. Two meter focal length and more provide better images but require a massive and rugged mount. Therefore, we slowly work our way ahead into the first photo night and focus on globular star clusters. When we for the first time see one in the eyepiece, we understand the name: Like a snowball of thousands of suns it is clearly to distinguished from the surrounding stars. Table 3 shows a list of globular star clusters from the Messier list [1].

Object	Brightness [mag]	Viewing angle
M2	6,3	16'
M3	6,2	18'
M5	6,65	23'
M10	6,6	20'
M13	5,8	20'
M15	6,2	18'
M22	5,5	32'
M92	6,3	14'

Table 4: Easy to observe globular star clusters [1].

The brightness in table 4 is measured by a specification, in which a smaller number means a brighter object. The viewing angle gives a measure of the size of the cluster in the eyepiece. Stellarium offers a tool to check the appearance of the object in the eyepiece, which Kstars does not offer. The selection of globular clusters in table 4 is restricted to those with a brightness 7 or smaller (brighter) and viewing angles over 10'. Thus, these objects are clearly visible even in small telescopes.

To test whether the object can be seen today in our environment, we are looking for it with the menu item "*Pointing |Find object*" or by clicking on the small binocular icon in the upper left menu bar. Then we choose "globular clusters" for the type filter and/or enter the name of a globular cluster in the name filter. Either the object is visible, then the FOV symbol moves to the corresponding point on the map and you can decide whether the object will be visible or hidden by trees or houses. Otherwise the object might be below the horizon. Then you will see nothing but green ground.

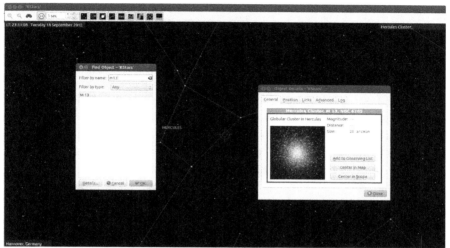

Figure 13: The globular cluster M13 is centered in the map, marked by the red FOV-symbol (Telrad finder). The details window shows astronomical details, including an image.

In figure 13 you can see that I have selected M13 from the list of globular clusters. A right click on the the map opens the context menu:

- A click on "Details" opens the detail window with a photo of the object.
- "Center and track" moves the object in the center of the map and keeps it there while time goes on.
- "Add to observation wish list" does what it says.

In the "*Settings | FOV symbols*" menu you can choose different viewfinder symbols (Here: red circles for Telrad finder) to mark the location of M13. As M13 at this time and location is located far to the west (SW), my telescope would just look into my bedroom. So I better look for another object. M15 would be well visible in the south. So I take M15 into my watch list, while I click "Add to observation wish list".

We repeat the tagging for all the objects that we have planned for that night. To save some work, let's put all objects from table 4 to the watchlist. So before dusk, we have completed the watchlist.

A bit more convenient is the setup wizard. With active observation wish list (Tools | Observing list) click on WUT (What's Up Tonight). Unfortunately, just for globular clusters Kstars 2.0.0 under Ubuntu 12.04 LTS are not accessible due to a bug: All globular clusters are stored without their brightness. As the WUT tool needs the brightness as a selection criterion, it fails just for globular clusters. Fortunately, the "Add object" tool (see figure 13) is nearly as useful as the WUT tool.

Once the selection process is finished, you have the observation wish list ready. Now you can go further setting up the session plan (figure 14).

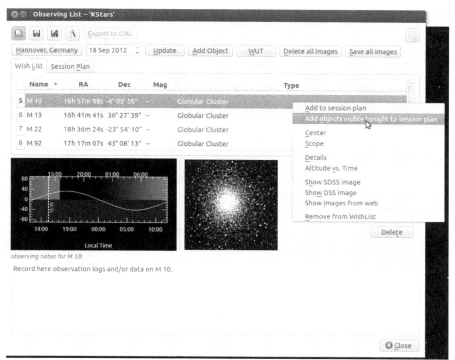

Figure14: All visible objects from the Wish List are added to the session plan in one single step.

Just mark all objects and then right click on one of them. Choose "Add objects visible tonight to session plan" in order to have all objects in the session plan.

Once done, you can see the visible objects in the session plan, together with a scheduling, when the object is best observed (highest above horizon). Now you know which objects when to look for this night. Good luck!

In the afternoon with Stellarium

The same scenario with Stellarium. By pushing the key "7" we stop the clock. Then we enter time and date in the corresponding window (F5). The date should be OK, but the time must be selected for the setup of the mount.

First, we check the location of Polaris at this time (figure 15). Pressing the "E" key, we turn on the equatorial coordinate grid to see where Polaris is located near the north celestial pole (NCP). Press F3 to find Polaris and center. We get the location of Polaris (figure 15) and as described in the Kstars section, we can use the polar finder scope to align the mount parallel to the earth axis.

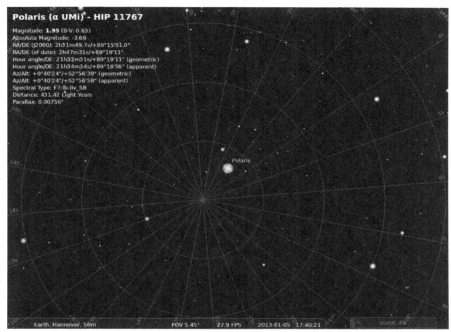

Figure 15: Polaris is located near the NCP. Inversion in the NCP gives the eyepiece view of Polaris in the polar finder scope.

Now we check the visibility of the globular star clusters from table 4. "F3" activates the search window. First let's look for M13.

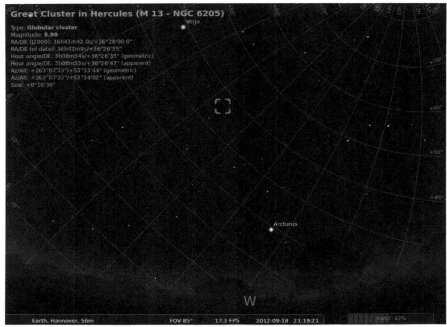

Figure 16: The globular cluster M13 is good visible in the west.

On the 18.9.2012 at 21:19 (MEST), M13 is good to see in the west, high enough above horizon (figure 16). So we put it on the list of observable objects. Unfortunately Stellarium does not support an observation list in a sophisticated manner like Kstars: We just have to use paper and pencil, just like with all other objects we want to observe.

The great advantage of Stellarium is the simulation of telescopes, eyepieces and cameras. This allows us to see the object like it will appear on the image sensor of your camera or in the eyepiece of your telescope. With "CTRL-O" you switch the eyepiece view on/off. In figure 17, you can preview how M13 will be visible through an 40mm eyepiece in an ETX-90 telescope.

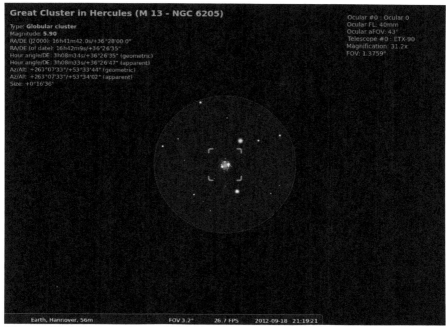

Figure 17: M13 seen in an ETX-90 telescope with an f=40mm eyepiece.

Once you configured your cameras, telescopes and eyepieces within Stellarium, you can preview an exact image of what is seen in the eyepiece and recorded on your image sensor. Figure 18 shows M13 how it would be recorded on the image sensor of an EOS 450D camera. Again, "Ctrl-O" allows to choose from your telescopes, cameras and eyepieces. How to configure your hardware is topic of the next chapter.

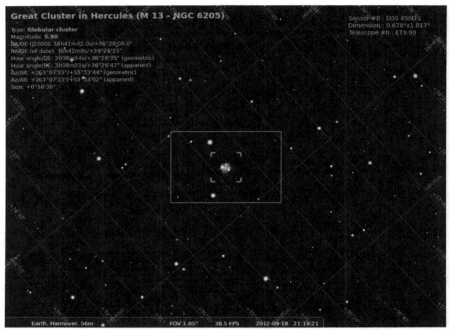

Figure 18: M13 on the image sensor of an EOS 450D camera at the end of an ETX-90 telescope.

Configuring your hardware in Stellarium

Configuration menu (F2)

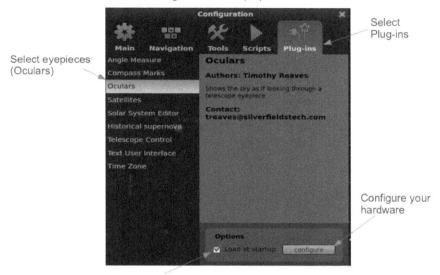

Start the eyepieces plug-in with the program

Figure 19: The configuration of your hardware starts in the configuration menu of Stellarium with "F2".

After pressing "F2", the configuration menu starts. The tab "Plug-Ins" accesses the eyepieces script called "Oculars" (figure 19). A mouse click on "configure" opens the configuration dialogue for telescopes, eyepieces and image sensors (figure 20).

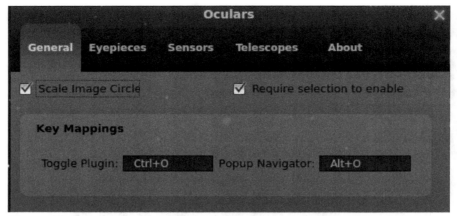

Figure 20: The general part of the Oculars setup remains untouched.

The general part of the Oculars setup remains untouched. A click on the tab „Eyepieces" leads to the setup for eyepieces (figure 21).

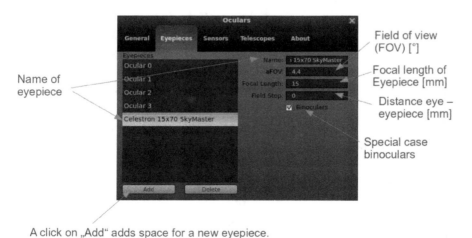

A click on „Add" adds space for a new eyepiece.

Figure 21: After clicking on "Add", you can enter the data of an eyepiece.

Figure 21 shows the data of the eyepieces, already available in Stellarium. You can enter your own eyepieces after clicking on the "Add" button. Then enter the fields on the right side.

The field entry of "aFOV" will limit the field of view on the screen, once you activate the oculars view with CTRL-O. So you can preview the effect of a wide field eyepiece vs. a normal field eyepiece.

Together with the focal length of a telescope, the focal length of the eyepiece determines the total magnification of your telescope (See chapter _Magnification_). Once you select an object, the calculated FOV from the total magnification of the selected telescope and eyepiece is used to show the astronomical object as you would see it in the telescope through the eyepiece.

Next, we add the cameras we are using to take photos. These are entered as "sensors" in the configuration menu (figure 22).

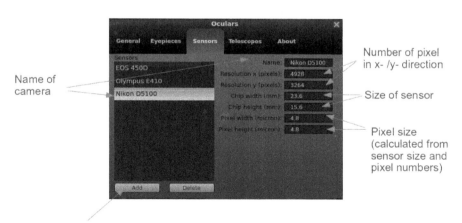

Figure 22: Entering a new camera starts with "Add". The data are stored in the right fields. Except the pixel size, all data are taken from the camera manual.

The camera EOS 450D is already given. Other cameras are added by pressing the "Add" button in figure 22. All data are taken from the camera's manual.

Only the pixel size is calculated by the equation:

$$p_{x/y} = \frac{c_{x/y}}{n_{x/y}}$$

Here are:

- $p_{x/y}$ the x- or y-pixel size
- $c_{x/y}$ the size of the sensor in x- or y- direction
- $n_{x/y}$ the corresponding pixel numbers.

Finally the hardware configuration is finished with the telescope data entry (figure 23).

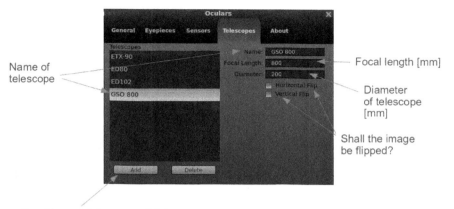

Name of
telescope

Focal length [mm]

Diameter
of telescope
[mm]

Shall the image
be flipped?

To add a new telescope, click here.

Figure 23: After adding a new telescope, the data are input on the right side.

Depending on your demand, you can instruct Stellarium to view the object either completely flipped (as seen through most telescopes) partially flipped (as seen through newtonian reflectors) or not flipped (as seen by naked eye). Normally a beginner is more confused by these options, so I deselect them.

Once you entered all data, just close the window. The configuration is saved and can be activated by the key combination CTRL-O. But before you can do so, you first have to select an object. Figure 24 shows the globular cluster M22 after selection, followed by CTRL-O. Using the ALT-O key combination you can select the eyepiece and / or the telescope. Press again the key combination CTRL-O to switch between ocular view and standard view back and forth.

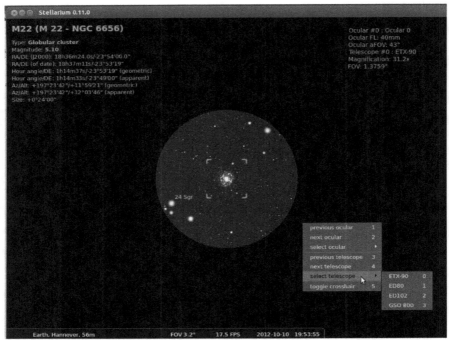

Figure 24: After selecting the globular cluster M22 and activating CTRL-O, you see the ocular view of M22. Pressing ALT-O allows to change telescope and ocular (eyepiece).

If you prefer the camera view of the object, you have to use ALT-O before switching to the ocular view (figure 25).

Figure 25: In the normal view you can switch to the camera view with ALT-O.

The first entry in the list of telescopes and cameras will be used. In this case it was the EOS 450D camera and the ETX-90 telescope (figure 26). Pressing again ALT-O allows to change the hardware or toggle back to normal view.

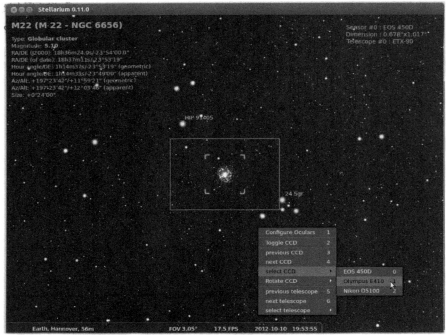

Figure 26: The sensor view was activated using ALT-O. Then ALT-O allows to select the sensor and telescope or toggle back to normal view.

Taking photos

The list of objects is made, the night is dark and the sky is clear. The mount is aligned using the polar finder scope as described using either Kstars or Stellarium. The alignment procedure of the GOTO mount is finished, so the GOTO mount knows where it is looking at and you have a bright reference star in the eyepiece. Now replace the eyepiece with the camera and set the camera into manual mode, select highest sensitivity level and set the shutter to the longest exposure time before bulb mode. This is normally 30s. Switch to live mode if possible or use the optical viewfinder to focus the camera manually on the reference star. Do this carefully and use the strongest magnification in live view possible. Then fix the focus carefully. Make sure the focus cannot move, because you will not be able to control the focus while photographing the astronomical objects on your list.

Now select the first entry from the list of objects and enter its name into the GOTO control. The mount swivels to the first object. Here we go with the pictures. The first photo will probably not be correctly centered. Repeat a photo with slightly corrected position, using the arrow keys of the GOTO mount. Once centered, do at least 10 photos of the same object, before you swivel onto the next object.

If you photographed near a city, the image will have a very bright background. Our object is hard to detect. Do not panic, we have the GIMP to improve the image. Nevertheless, the object in the center of the image should be recognized, even if only very weak.

After we photographed an object, we do not immediately swing to the next object but look for a reference star in the vicinity of the object. Which is centered again. Then we swing to the object. The reason is the usually not so good adjustment, so that the wanted object shows a large displacement when the move is too long. It might even be outside the field of view of the image sensor. And as the object itself is not visible in the live view mode of the camera, a stop at the neighbour reference star helps correcting the displacement. The reference star should be so bright, that it is visible in the live view.

After all objects on the nights wish list have been photographed, we end with a full memory chip and go to bed.

Postprocessing of the images

Now we start with the week of post processing. Yes, it is a time consuming process. And you should do it in several steps in order not to lose precious data. Here comes the textual description. A full color image based description follows later. Experienced GIMP users will prefer this text based description, inexperienced GIMP users might want to step over to the image based description.

Save your images on hard disk

1. **Saving with system.** I use the folder ~/Images/Astronomy for all astro images. Each object gets its own folder in there. In that folder I create a folder for every observation night. For example, all photos made on 18.9.2012 from M13 go into the folder ~/Images/Astronomy/M13/18.9.2012. As you have taken photos from several objects in a night, you will repeat the procedure of creating folders for every object you have made photos of. Then you copy all original untouched photos from the camera chip into the corresponding folders on your hard disk.

Processing the individual images with GIMP

2. **Subtraction of the background.** Every single image is loaded individually into GIMP. Then the color pipette is used to select the color of a background point. A background point might be any point in the image, which is considered to contain no data of stars or the object itself. Clicking on this

point with the pipette (color picker tool) sets the foreground color.

3. **Creating a new subtracting plane.** Create a new plane with the selected foreground color. Set the modus of the new plane to "Subtraction". The background of the image should now turn to black. But as normally also parts of the object fall below visibility, set the subtraction from 100% to 90% or less. Let your eyes decide the amount of subtraction.

4. **Saving the processed image as intermediate result.** The original image has a name given by the camera, like DSC_XYZ.jpg, where XYZ are numbers. This name is still shown in the GIMP header line. I now save the processed image as OBJECT_XYZ.jpg, i.e. I replace the camera's name of the image (DSC or whatever) by the object's name. If the image shows M13, I save the image for example as M13_123.jpg, if the original name was DSC_123.jpg. Then the relation to the original image is kept.

5. **Repeat steps 2. - 4. for all photos of the same object.** In the end we have the same number of intermediate images as original images in the corresponding folder.

The figures 27-31 show the same steps using the images of the Andromeda nebula M31, taken with my Nikon D5100 at ISO6400 with my ED102 refractor on the HEQ5 mount with 30s exposure time without auto guiding.

Summing up individually processed images

6. **Loading the median number processed image.** There is a time gap of some minutes between the first and the last image taken. Once the mount is never exactly aligned to the

earth axis, the object moved a bit in each image. So we load the median number image into GIMP. This image is now our reference image. We switch to 100% view (1:1) in order to work pixel precise in the following steps.

7. **Loading the next image as *"new plane"*.** We now add a new plane with the another image of the object in the same date folder. We now have two layers in the same GIMP image. The newly loaded image is on top of the first loaded background image and therefore covers the background image.

8. **Setting transparency to 50%.** To make both images equally visible, set the transparency to 50%. Now the new image in the foreground is as visible as the old one in the background. Now we can see the displacement between the two images.

9. **Select the move tool and move the new plane.** Once you select the move tool, you can move the selected plane. It is important to move the newly loaded plane image, not the original image in the background. Make sure that you have set the zoom factor to 100% (1:1) in order to control the movement pixelwise.

10. **Switch off new plane.** This step prepares the repetition of steps 6. - 11.

11. **Change plane mode to *"Addition"*.** The adjusted new plane will be added later on to all other layers. This causes a better exposition of the image, as the light of each plane is added to the other ones. Simultaneously the image gets a noise reduction, as the summation acts like averaging.

12. **Repeating steps 6. - 11. for all images of the same object in the same date folder.** At the end of the process, we have at least 10 precisely aligned image layers, one for each intermediate image. All layers are in the "addition" mode. You should make sure that always only two layers are visible
    a. The background plane.

b. The plane you are actual working on. All other layers should not be visible. This increases the operation speed.

13. **Save the image in the GIMP format.** There is a lot of work in the image you now created. To save it, make sure you save as a new image in the GIMP format with the ending *.xcf. Following the proposal of the text before, you would save this image as ~/Images/Astronomy/M13/18.9.2012/M13.xcf. There is no information loss using the xcf-format, which results in a high volume output. 30MB for one stacked GIMP image is nothing extraordinary. The main work is done and we have saved it. What follows is fine tuning, which is still very time consuming.

14. **Switch on all layers.** As we make all layers visible, GIMP is becoming slower and slower with each added plane. Simultaneously you will observe the image getting brighter and brighter with every plane you switch on. Bright stars show up overexposed very soon. Thats the reason for the next step.

15. **Tuning the contribution of the layers.** Originally all layers are adding their pixel values to 100% to the pixel in the visible image. Now we reduce the contribution of the individual layers. If we have 10 images in the different layers and set the contribution to 10%, the resulting image has the same brightness as the original images each pixel value is multiplied by 0.1 before it is added to the sum picture, but the noise is reduced. Setting the contribution to a value between 10% and 100% controls the brightening (increase of exposure time) of the image. So we have a tool to control the exposure time after exposition. For astro images normally the rule is: The longer the exposure time, the better. But unfortunately the resulting summary image is still caught in the 8-bit frame of the standard image formats. We

need to use compound technologies like HDR or stacking and painting to reduce the burden of 8-bit dynamics in astronomical photos. So we might risk to overexpose bright image parts in order to get the more interesting darker parts of the object better visible later. I will explain that in the chapter Fotoxx, which does just that. Now we try to set the contribution of the layers in such a way, that the resulting summary image shows the wanted structures clearly. We risk some overexposure, which we cure later. In order not to over weigh the background plane (it is just another plane like all others), we change their status to "Addition" and set the contribution to the same value as the other layers. Then we add a new black background plane in the very background of   all   other   layers.

All in all we control two effects:

   a. As we reduce the contribution of layers, the image gets darker, as we increase the contribution of layers, the image gets brighter.

   b. We can fine tune the quality by increasing the contribution of good images and decreasing the contribution of images with some problems (e.g. a bit shaken). Let your eye decide.

16. **Save the fine tuned summary image.** You might later on refine the image by starting tuning work from this image. You might prefer a new name for the tuned image like M13_1.xcf for the first variant of your fine tuning work. In any case use GIMP's lossless xcf format.

17. **Save as JPG.** The xcf format is readable only by GIMP, but you may want to upload your images in the web. Therefore it is time to save a copy of your fine tuned image as JPG. This is the version you might also want to print.

18. **Fine tuning of the JPG image.** There are still some unused parameters, we can modify to work out details of the object:

a. In all layers of the summary image are still some leftovers of background illumination. In the summary image these also sum up and may lead to a considerable background illumination. Even worse: The background is normally not equally distributed but has a gradient: More background illumination near horizon, less in zenith. This will come up more visible in the summary image and therefore is subject to our postprocessing of the summary image. We now can remove gradients by the same technique as mentioned before, with a slight modification: We create a new white plane and fill it with the gradient, we create with the pipette tool.

   i. Select the foreground color FG with the pipette at a bright background location.

   ii. Select the background color BG with the pipette at a dark background location.

   iii. Select the needed gradient:

   1. Linear gradient for horizon-zenith type of gradient.

   2. Circular gradient for gradients caused by bad optics.

   iv. Fill the white plane with the gradient tool from the FG point to the BG point. You now have the gradient plane.

   v. Subtract the gradient plane from the background plane.

   vi. Modify the contribution of the gradient plane to your needs.

b. Modification of the gradient curve. With the menu entry "*Color | Curves*" you can change the gradation curve. Selecting this tool from the main menu, shows up the histogram of the image, i.e. the distribution of pixels ordered by brightness. You can use the curve for luminance (i.e. the total brightness) or separate for red green or blue. Lifting up the curve makes the pixel below that curve part brighter, pushing down the curve makes the corresponding pixels darker. As the curve is flexible like an elastic ribbon, you can make dark pixels brighter and bright pixels darker.

Once you have the curve tool active, a right click on that part of the image with fine details marks the region in the histogram. If you want the details more crispy, make the gradation curve around this mark steeper rising. Be sure to have the preview button activated, then you can directly control the effect of your work.

The extensive description suggests that no more than a single photo can be edited in one afternoon. Probably less.

Now follows the same description as above, but with images.

Image processing explained by example images

Figure 27: Step 1 - One original image of M31 is loaded. You can see the light pollution in an urban environment. The pipette tool is used to set the foreground color.

Click on background here...

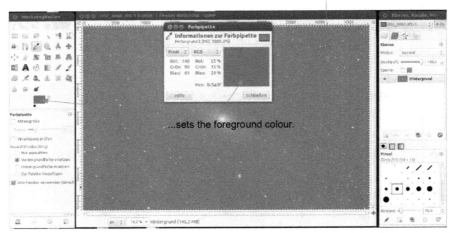

...sets the foreground colour.

Figure 28: Step 2 - A mouse click with the pipette tool to a background point sets the foreground colour.

Create a new layer with the foreground colour.

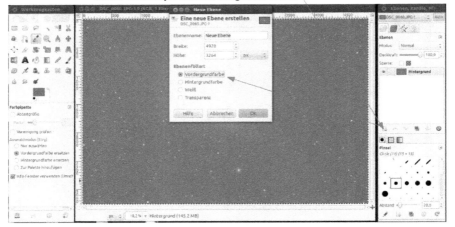

Figure 29: Step 3 - Create a new layer with foreground colour.

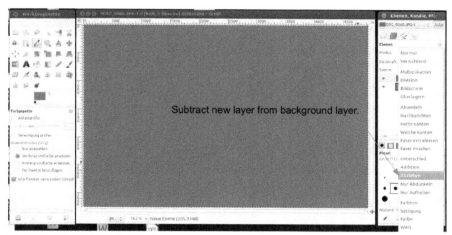

Figure 30: Step 4 - The newly created layer is subtracted from the background layer: Switch the layer mode from "Normal" to "Subtract".

Reduce opacity to 90 (less aggressive).

Figure 31: Step 5 - Reduce the opacity to 90 (%) or less to make the subtraction of the background less aggressive. The background illumination is nearly gone. The image is now saved as M31_XYZ.jpg, where XYZ is the original numbering from the camera.

You have to repeat the above procedure for all images in the same object/date-folder. Once done you have 10 images of the same object with the background illumination (light pollution) removed.

Illustrated description of the summation

Here come steps 6. - 18. with illustrating example images.

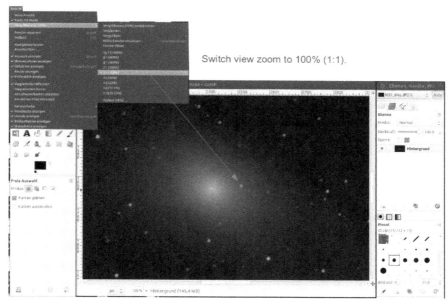

Switch view zoom to 100% (1:1).

Figure 32: Step 6 - Load the median image and switch to 1:1 view (100%). This allows pixel precise working.

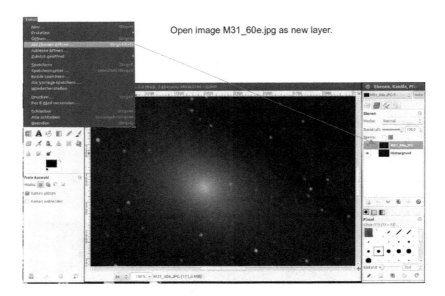

Figure 33: Step 7 - A new image is loaded into a new layer of the same image. It pops up with the name in the layer dialogue.

Reducing the opacity of the upper layer to 50 (%) makes both images visible.

Figure 34: Step 8 - Reducing the opacity of the upper layer to 50 makes both images visible. You can see the drift between both photos.

The move tool moves the active layer and results in aligned layers.

Figure 35: Step 9 - After moving the active layer with the move tool, both layers are aligned pixel by pixel.

All images are added by 22% to the black background (new layer).

All images are loaded, aligned and visible.

A new created black layer
serves as the background layer
to which all others are added.

Figure 36: Step 10 - All images are added to the black background layer. The addition is limited to 22% of the pixel value in order to avoid over exposure in the middle part. Note that the image is no longer in the 100% zoom but fills the frame.

This result is saved now as M31.xcf. This file contains all information about layers, layer mode and opacity and is the base file for fine tuning. In addition the same image is also saved as M31.JPG, which is a file usable in all image applications, inclusive web pages. This file is the target for fine tuning as described in the following chapter.

Enhancing details by changing the gradation curve

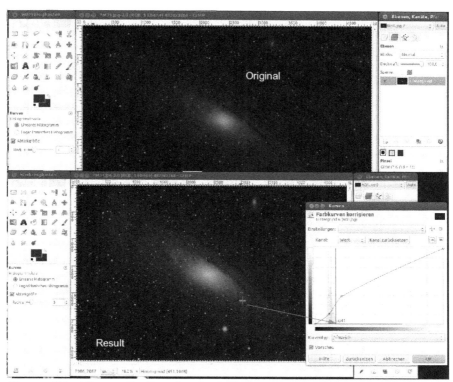

Figure 37: After activating the tool "Colors | Curve" the gradation curve pops up. A click into the nebula (red cross) marks the pixels brightness value (41). Making the gradation curve a bit steeper here causes an improvement in the faint nebula structures.

Removing a background gradient

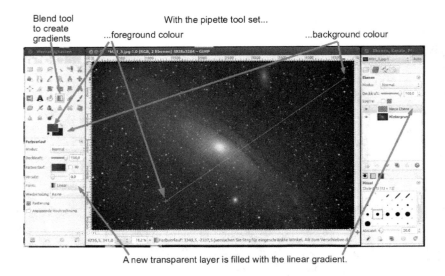

Blend tool to create gradients

With the pipette tool set...

...foreground colour

...background colour

A new transparent layer is filled with the linear gradient.

Figure 38: A linear background gradient is removed. In a first step, the pipette selects the foreground colour, Second the background colour is set. Then a new layer is created and filled with the linear gradient.

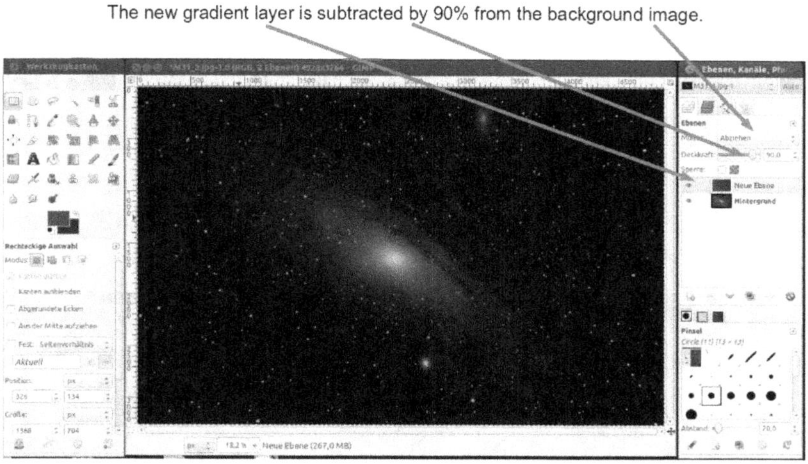

The new gradient layer is subtracted by 90% from the background image.

Figure 39: The result of the gradient subtraction is quite impressive. The ugly light pollution is gone.

Post processing of images with Fotoxx

Occasionally astronomical objects show enormous differences in brightness, which an image sensor (CCD or CMOS) cannot handle due to its linear brightness characteristic. As an example, we have a look at an image of the great Orion nebula M42 (figure 40), taken with the GSO 800 mirror and the Nikon D5100 with 400ISO and 30s exposure time.

Figure 40: The sum of 16 images of M42 with 400ISO and 30s exposure time taken by the Nikon D5100 camera in the primary focus of the GS= 800 Newton mirror (f=800mm, d=200mmm). All images are aligned and added by 20% as described in the last chapter.

While the gas tail structures become very good visible by the summation of images, the center of the nebula, the trapezoid, is overexposed.

Each architectural photographer knows about this problem when photographing interior spaces: The window part is hopelessly overexposed, the dark fireplace is sinking in the shade.

This problem is solved by a digital photo technique called HDR (High Dynamic Range). This technique uses two or more photos of the same object, one with the right exposure for the dark regions, one with the right exposure for the light regions and may be some more for the midlight regions. Then these photos are mixed together using profile curves. The darker parts finally come from the image with the long exposure, while the light parts are taken from the short exposed image with the light image details. The result is then compiled into one HDR image. Fotoxx is making this procedure quite easy, once you have the photos aligned with GIMP.

Creating an HDR image with Fotoxx

The preparation of the HDR image with Fotoxx is a 4 step process:
1. Start the HDR composite under the menu item "*Combine | High dynamic range*".
2. Selection of images for the composite. A minimum of 2 and a maximum of 9 images can be incorporated into an HDR composite.
3. Modify the profile curves of the images involved.
4. Save the final image.

Preparation (Creation of 2 images for HDR use)

As the creation of the HDR image requires 2 different exposed images, we create these before we start Fotoxx and dive into the

HDR creation process. We start with the aligned GIMP image of the M42 nebula (figure 40) called M42.xcf and load it in GIMP. As we need two images for the HDR composite, we take the summed up image as one of them. So we save M42.xcf as M42_a.jpg. This is the image, where the dark parts are well exposed, but the trapezoid is over exposed. Next we switch off all layers except one (the base layer) and set this layer to normal mode and 100 opacity. The image is now very dark, the gas tail is nearly invisible, but the trapezoid turns out well exposed. This image is saved as M42_b.jpg (figure 41). Now we have two images, one with good visible gas tail, one with the good visible trapezoid.

Figure 41: A single layer of M42.xcf is visible, all others are switched off. The mode of the layer is set to "normal" and the opacity set to 100. This image is saved as M42_b.jpg.

Starting Fotoxx (Step 1)

You start Fotoxx and click on the menu item *"Combine | High dynamic range"* in Fotoxx to start the HDR creation process.

Selection of images (Step 2)

After starting the HDR creation (step 1) with *"Combine | High dynamic range"*, the two images, M42_a.jpg and M42_b.jpg, are selected and loaded. Fotoxx tries to find any shifts in the images and to align them. As we did the alignment procedure in GIMP manually, there might remain some shifts, which Fotoxx tries to remove. This is a very cpu-intensive process that requires several minutes on older PCs. During this process, the critical areas of the image will be displayed as red areas. In the bottom of the image appear status information and the keyword BUSY. After completion of the alignment work, a preview of the HDR image is shown.

Modifying the profile curves (Step 3)

How the HDR image is composed from the original images is controlled by the profile curves. After completion of the alignment procedure, the proposed standard profile curves are just linear. The result is in most cases not really bad, but you should have in mind, that the selection follows a summation rule: The pixel value in the HDR image is calculated from the pixel values in the individual images by multiplying the pixel value in image A with the profile curve A value and added to the corresponding product in image B:

$$p_{HDR}(x) = f_A(x) * p_A(x) + f_B(x) * p_B(x)$$

with:

- $p_{HDR}(x)$: Pixel value at position x in the HDR image.

- $f_A(x)$: Value of profile curve image A at position x.

- $p_A(x)$: Pixel value of image A at position x.

- $f_B(x)$: Value of profile curve image B at position x.

- $p_B(x)$: Pixel value of image B at position x.

In order to get the well exposed tail of M42 in M42_a.jpg not destroyed by M42_b.jpg and vice versa for the information of the trapezoid part of the image, the profile curves should have clear edges. Left of the edge, the dark part is taken from M42_a.jpg, right of the edge, the bright part is taken from M42_b.jpg. Figure 42 shows an HDR preview of the two images, created by two modified profile curves.

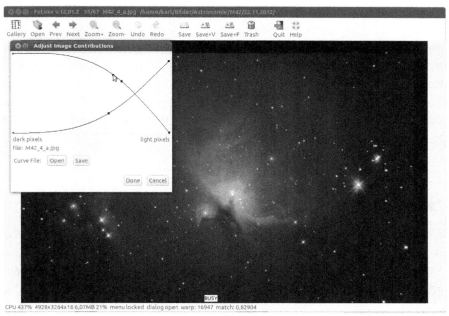

Figure 42: The HDR composite preview from the images M42_4_a.jpg (good visibility of the nebula environment) and M42_4_b.jpg (good visibility of the trapezoid). The profile curves show clearly the corresponding contributions. Playing with the profile curves can give surprising results. Just try it.

In this picture, both the trapezoid and the gaseous nebula is easily recognizable. The two profile curves (one for each image) govern the content of each picture in the HDR preview. The lighter pixels are primarily from the dark M42_4_b.jpg, the darker pixels come from the image M42_4_a.jpg.

The modification of the profile curves with the mouse (In the beginning, the profile curves lines) essentially determined the look of the HDR image. It is a good investment to spend a lot of time for fine tuning the profile curves.

Saving the HDR image (Step 4)

If you are happy with the composition, the image is saved as a new image. This is done either via the menu *"File | Save to new file"* or by the button *"Save+F"* . In both cases you can determine the location and the image format. Usually you will prefer the * jpg. or *.png format, but also the very memory consuming TIFF format is offered, the latter even with 16Bit/Pixel. If the images are shown on the web, jpg or png is your choice.

Stack and paint with Fotoxx

There is another technique offered by Fotoxx, which is also useful or even more useful, once the range of overexposure is limited to a small area, like in the M42 image above. Again we use the two images M42_a.jpg and M42_b.jpg, created as described in the chapter before. But this time we choose the Stack/Paint technique:

1. Start of procedure by *"Combine | Stack / Paint"*.
2. Selection of images for the compound (M42_a.jpg, M42_b.jpg).
3. Painting the final image from the individual images.
4. Saving the resulting compound image.

You can see, that the steps are quite similar to those for an HDR compound, except step 1, where a different procedure is selected.

Step 3 is that one, which has to be described in more detail, the other ones should be clear from the previous description.

Selection of image for painting (Step 3)

After the alignment procedure, the image is calculated by the average or median of the pixel values in the individual image components. This causes some kind of contrast reduction, which is not the wanted result. Instead we wanted the dark parts as in the bright image and the bright parts like in the dark image (figure 43). Here you can see:

1. The image is calculated by the average of the two contributing images.
2. In the left upper corner you find the control window for painting. You can select any of the contributing images and the size of the painting brush. With this brush you paint the content of the selected contributing image to the location of the brush, once you press the left mouse button. This means, that the calculated average pixel value is replaced by the original pixel value in the selected image under the painting brush.
3. In the compound image, the mouse pointer indicates the actual image range foreseen for painting with the content of the selected contributing image.

In our case, we paint the complete image with M42_4_a.jpg and then the trapezoid with M42_4_b.jpg. The result is shown in figure 44.

Figure 43: The image shows the preview of the Stack / Paint compound image. The contributing images are M42_a.jpg and M_42_b.jpg.

Figure 44: The result of the Stack / Paint procedure shows both well exposed: The faint nebula region from M42_a.jpg and the trapezoid center from M42_b.jpg.

Example images

You will need a high quality print book to see astronomical images in a good quality. But an eBook is not the right place to publish photos. As those who buy eBooks normally have access to the Internet, you will find a selection of my images here [2]. All images are created in the light polluted environment of the city of Hannover, Germany. Just from my backyard. What really surprises is the fact, that under such bad conditions even weak gas nebula like NGC7000 could be photographed.

Advanced techniques

INDI

Installation of INDI drivers

1. You have to tell your software-center the location of your software repository. Do this with the command **sudo add-apt-repository ppa:mutlaqja/ppa** in a terminal window. From now on, the UBUNTU software-center has the INDI drivers available.
2. Trigger an update of the software repository with the command **sudo apt-get update** in a terminal window. Now the software-center knows the latest versions of the INDI drivers.
3. Install INDI with a software-center (e.g. synaptic).
   a) **Indi-bin**: This is the core driver. It offers hooks for all components of the INDI system.
   b) In case of using a camera with the INDI driver, you have to install **indi-gphoto-ccd**. This is the driver for Canon DSLR. Other cameras cannot be used.

Once you have installed the INDI drivers, you can start the integration of the drivers into Kstars and Stellarium.

Access to the serial interface

The GOTO mount is accessible by a serial interface (RS-232). This kind of interface was standard at modem times, but is completely out-fashioned today. Most computers do not have one any more. Instead computers have USB interfaces. In order to add a RS-232 interface to your computer, you must have an USB-RS232 converter cable, which is easily available in any computer store.

Now remember that it was dangerous to allow people to have access to a modem, because this could make explode your telephone cost. This is the reason, why only root and all members of the group *dialout* had access to the serial interface. In order to get access to the GOTO mount at the other end of the serial line, we have to set ourself as member into the dialout group. Figure 45 shows the corresponding entry in my /etc/group file. Just add your login after the colon. To do that, the easiest way is to start the Midnight Commander (mc), a Norton Commander clone for Linux, as root with the command *sudo mc* in a terminal window, look for the file group in the folder /etc and load it for modification. Then add you login to the group dialout and save the file. In case you cannot find, modify or save the file, you have probably not started mc as root with the sudo command.

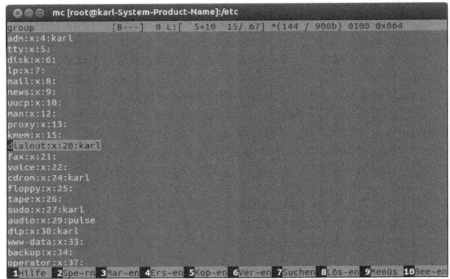

*Figure 45: In the file /etc/group your login has to be after the group name dialout. You can only modify this file as root. The easiest way is opening the file with **sudo mc** for writing.*

Adding INDI to Kstars

You should now place your mount aside your computer and connect the RS-232 serial line of the mount with the USB-RS232 converter connected with your computer. You do not have to make a full setup with optics and camera, just place the mount near the computer and switch it on, no optics or cameras on it. Do the alignment procedure for any virtual star and make the mount believe it is looking at it.

Now start Kstars and start the device manager (Devices | Devicemanager). There you select the telescope type, start the INDI service and configure the serial interface with your first service start. Finally you start the connection. If everything is running well, the telescope pointer pops up in the Kstars display at the location your scope points to (figure 46).

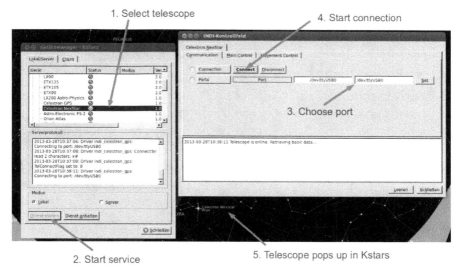

Figure 46: The easy installation under Kstars is done in 4 steps. As a result, the telescope marker pops up a the position, the telescope points at.

Once the connection is working, you may click on another object in the sky with the right button of your mouse. The opening context menu shows an entry, which moves the scope to the selected object (figure 47).

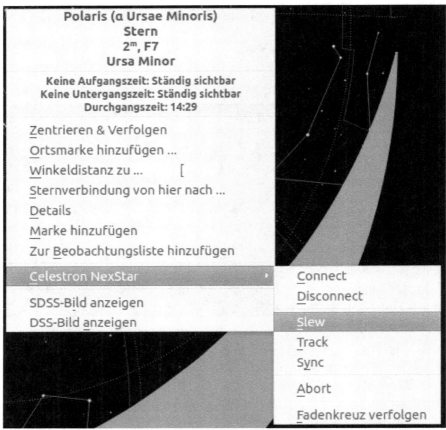

*Figure 47: Polaris was chosen with a right mouse click. Activating **slew** moves the scope to this star.*

Adding INDI to Stellarium

Use the **plugins** flag at the configuration window [F2] to select the Telescope Control (figure 48).

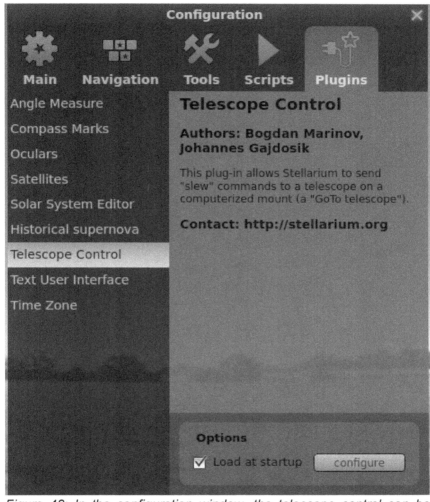

Figure 48: In the configuration window, the telescope control can be loaded at start time. The first start needs a configuration.

Once you click on ***configure***, you will be able to add a new scope (figure 49).

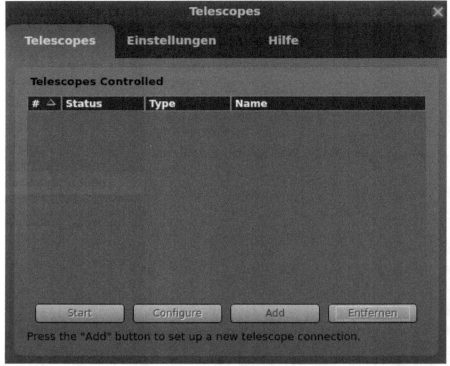

*Figure 49: No scope is available. A mouse click on **Add**, creates a new entry.*

Just click on **Add** to create a new entry for your scope (figure 50).

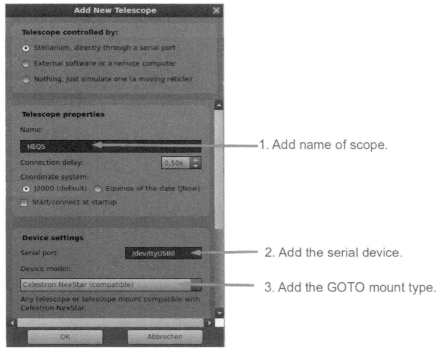

1. Add name of scope.

2. Add the serial device.

3. Add the GOTO mount type.

Figure 50: After adding the scope name, the serial device and the scope type, the configuration is finished.

Clicking on OK finished the configuration and the scope is ready to use in Stellarium (figure 51).

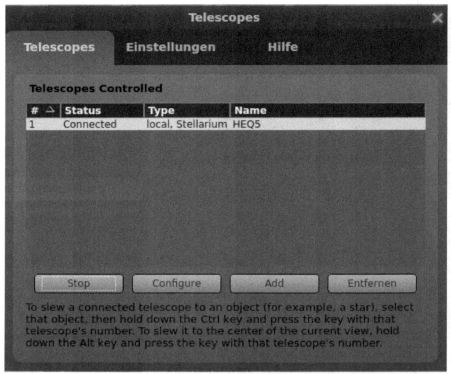

Figure 51: After configuration, you can use the scope. The communication is started with the start button, which changes after start to the stop button.

The connection is started by a mouse click on the **Start** button. Once the scope is connected, the Start button changes to the **Stop** button. Once you close the control window, the scope pointer pops up at the correct location (figure 52).

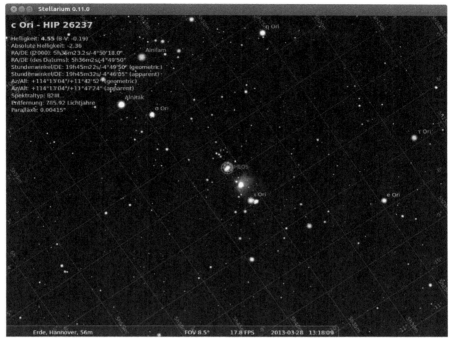

Figure 52: Once the scope is connected to the computer, the pointer with the name of the scope pops up at the correct location. Selecting a new object by mouse click makes the scope slew there, when STRG+1 (for the first and probably only scope) is pressed simultaneously.

To slew the scope to a new object, just mark the object with a mouse click. As usual, the name of the object appears in the upper left corner of the screen. Once you press simultaneously the Strg and the number 1 key, the scope slews to that object.

Gphoto2

gphoto2 [19] is a command line software, which uses the libgphoto library to access digital cameras. Whether the installation is useful for you depends on your camera. While the homepage mentions more than 1600 supported cameras, support in most cases simply means, that you can read the images directly from the cameras memory card. What we want is a bit more complicated: We want to control the cameras shutter. At the moment, this is possible only for Canon and Nikon DSLR cameras. The reason is not of technical nature. The manufacturers simply do not give information to programmers, and so only the most used DSLR are programmed by try and error. To profit from gphoto2, you must install the software and yourself try out if your camera is cooperating or not.

Installation

For installation use **Synaptic** or any other software manager in your main menu. Select **gphoto2** and install with a mouse click on **Apply** (figure 54).

After installation, gphoto2 is ready to use in a terminal window.

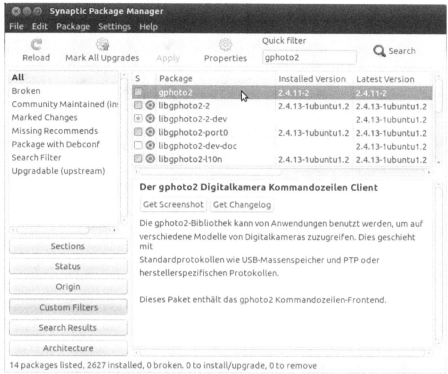

Figure 53: gphoto2 can be installed with Synaptic. You find Synaptic in the main menu.

Taking photos with gphoto2

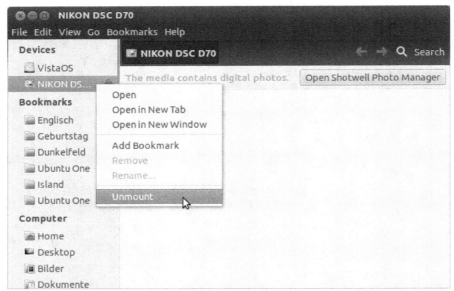

Figure 54: The context menu of the memory card of your camera allows unmounting it. This enables gphoto2 to exclusively communicate with the camera.

The camera is connected with your computer with the USB cable coming with your camera. Switch on the camera and a file manager window pops up (figure 54).

gphoto2 requires exclusive access to the camera, so the memory card must be unmounted from the computer system. To do this, right click on the memory card and choose **Unmount** from the context menu, as shown in figure 54.

Next open a terminal window. Use the cd command to change into that folder, where you would like the camera to deposit your photos. If you are not familiar with Linux/Unix commands, I recommend using **mc**, Midnight Commander, a Norton Commander clone. Once you arrived in the destination folder, you can issue a command to see if your camera is detected. If you used mc, you go to the terminal line by pressing Ctrl-O. Then type the following command:

gphoto2 -auto-detect

If your camera is detected, you can try to get 2 photos with your camera by typing the following command:

gphoto2 -I 1 -F 2 –capture-image-and-download

The meaning of the parameters:
- **-I**: The interval in seconds before the next frame is taken. In the example above, 1s delay was chosen.
- **-F**: The number of frames to take. In the example, two frames where ordered.
- **--capture-image-and-download**: This triggers taking the photos and after that downloading it into the target folder, from which you started the command. The camera settings where used.

Figure 55 shows the summary.

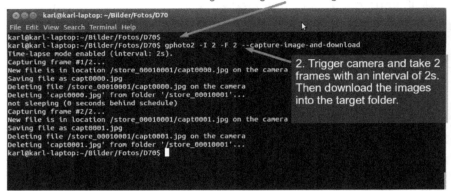

Figure 55: The command cd moves into the target folder. Here is the deposit location for the images. After reaching the destination folder, the gphoto2 command is triggered. In this example we order two photos with a delay of 2s.

The result are two photos in the destination folder (figure 56).

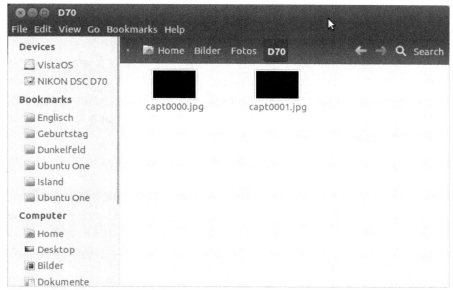

Figure 56: The successful gphoto2 command results in two photos in the destination folder.

Using several cameras simultaneously

As astrophotos need a long exposure time, it might be useful to trigger two ore more cameras (with different optics) at the same time. This is very easy: Just open one terminal window for each camera and then move into one target folder for each camera. The selection of the camera within the gphoto2 command is done with the parameter - -*camera=,* followed by the name of the camera, as gphoto2 detects it with the command **gphoto2 -auto-detect**. Just copy & paste the name from the output of the command after the **- - camera=** parameter in the command for triggering photos.

Darktable

I use darktable only as a trendy GUI for gphoto2. As many people feel unhappy with command line programs, this might be an acceptable solution. But darktable is a heavy load program, resulting in some slow work. A command line is much faster, once you know how to handle it.

Installation of darktable

You should not try to install darktable from your standard repository, until you are sure that you install the latest version. The development process has undergone some progress which you should profit from. So before installation, tell your software manager where to find the latest version:

1. Tell the software manager where to find the latest version. In a terminal window issue the command **sudo add-apt-repository** ppa:pmjdebruijn/darktable-release.
2. Get an update of the of the available software in that repository by issuing the command **sudo apt-get update** in a terminal window.
3. Now your software manager is able to install the latest version of darktable. Run the software manager and install darktable as usual.

Using darktable

I will not describe the full use of darktable. I still prefer the GIMP for all image manipulation issues as described in the above chapters. Instead I will focus on the *Tethering mode* which means just a nice GUI for using gphoto2.
After the start of darktable the program looks like in figure 57.

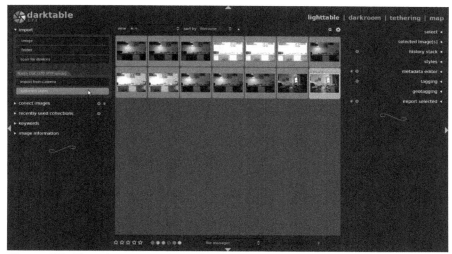

Figure 57: The startup window of darktable shows the detected camera on the left side. In the middle are the last taken photos in the target folder. In the right are the settings for manipulation of existing photos.

As said, I concentrate on tethering images with one of the detected cameras. A mouse click on the tethering register opens the camera control window (figure 58).

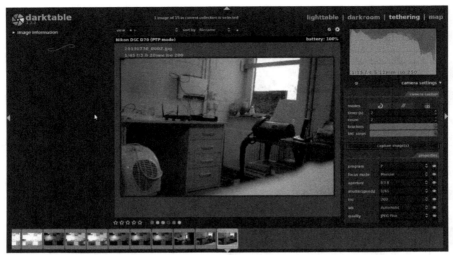

Figure 58: darktable in tethering mode. On the right side you can control the camera settings. You can take single exposures, series of exposures and bracketed exposures.

Darktable puts all taken images in a so called film roll. That is just the name of the file folder in the folder ~/Bilder/darktables. The concrete name of the file folder also contains the actual date and a so called job code. After choosing your own job code, you can create the corresponding folder by pressing the create button in the session part above the camera settings section on the right hand side.

Darktable just takes the settings of the camera (at least for Nikon DSLR) and shows them in the camera settings properties section. As a user you can now set the number of frames and the timer setting in the corresponding fields of the camera control section. A mouse click on the button *capture images* does just that. This is a more comfortable way of using gphoto2.

RawTherapee

Once you press the button of your camera, a complex computer program in the camera starts reading the binary information from the sensor chip, and processes these raw data in order to eliminate artefacts like noise, lens distortion, optic aberrations resulting from poor lenses or white color balance. At the end of the process, the image is corseted into 8 bit/color pixel to create a JPG image, while the sensor might have delivered up to 16 bit/color pixel information. The result is a loss of information.

To avoid this loss of information, the camera manufacturers offer for their high end cameras the option, not to save the processed JPG image, but the original sensor data. These data then are saved unprocessed (with all artefacts) in a RAW file. The ending of the RAW file varies by manufacturer (*.ORF is used by Olympus, *.NEF is used by Nikon,...), but the principle is always the same: Just readout the sensor data and save them unmodified in a file on the memory card. Most cameras offer to save the image in two versions: RAW and JPG. You should make use of this offer, until you are very experienced with processing a RAW file.

RawTherapee [21] is a software to take the RAW file from a lot of manufacturers and allows to manipulate the resulting image, like in a classical dark chamber. This is the reason for calling the manipulation process the "development" of the image. In fact, RawTherapee does not more but working on the sensor data, leaving the original data untouched. It just saves the manipulation parameters with the original data. So after manipulation of the image, the original sensor data remains untouched. The program causes no data loss, as the sensor data are calculated in floating point arithmetic. This is much better than the integer arithmetic which GIMP uses, as you create rounding errors with each manipulation step. Of course: At the end of the process, RawTherapee too has to create an 8 bit/color pixel JPG image, with the corresponding data loss. But during the whole manipulation process, this happens once, at the end of the process, not with each manipulation step.

Installation of RawTherapee

RawTherapee is available for Mac, Windows and Linux. I focus on the installation on Ubuntu LINUX 12.04. On [21] you find the corresponding ZIP archive. Ubuntu allows the installation directly from the software manager, but then you get an outdated version. You should download the LINUX archive and unpack the archive, then install the software to get the latest version running. For easy access, set a link to the installed software on the desktop. Then start the software from the desktop and not from the main menu, where the old version might be installed.

Working with RawTherapee

Assuming that you have at least 10 images/object in the RAW format and you want to develop them for later summing up with the GIMP. This is your workflow:
1. Start RawTherapee from the desktop (figure 59).
2. Activate the register *File browser* on the top left of the screen.
3. Open the folder with your RAW images with a mouse double click. The images are shown as thumbnails in the middle part of the screen.
4. Open the first image by a double click on it. The image now fills the whole middle part. The right side shows the control elements for the development process, including a histogram of the image.
5. Manipulate the development parameters to make the image suitable for further processing in GIMP. You will need some

practice an intuition to succeed. Just try! And remember: You do not destroy anything, as the original RAW file is not touched. Your are just changing (and later storing) development parameters. If you are lost, just reset to original values.

6. Once you have found a nice set of parameters, you save it for use with all other images of the same series. The second from left register in the right part of the screen allows to **save the profile**. If you copy the profile into the clipboard, you can easily paste it from there into the next image before closing the software.

7. Insert the image into the queue (the button with the gear pinion or [Ctrl+Q]). All images in the queue will be later developed into JPG or TIFF files.

8. Close the image by clicking on the diagonal cross near the filename at the upper part of the frame.

9. Repeat steps 4-8 for all usable images of the series. You can use the developed profile by simply getting the profile from the clipboard (right part of the screen, most right button). You should immediately get a usable image and put the image into the queue. After this step, all usable images should wait in the queue for processing into JPG or TIFF images.

10. Activate the queue by clicking on the register card **Queue** ([Ctrl-F3). You see all RAW files awaiting development in the middle part of the screen.

11. Select the folder to save your results. The proposal is to save the results in the subfolder **converted** of the actual image folder.

12. Select the file format of the developed file. JPG is the most common image format, but they are compressed with information loss. TIFF images are uncompressed and large, but without information loss.

13. Start processing by clicking the corresponding button. Image for image are now developed into the target file. After finished development, the RAW image disappears from the processing queue.

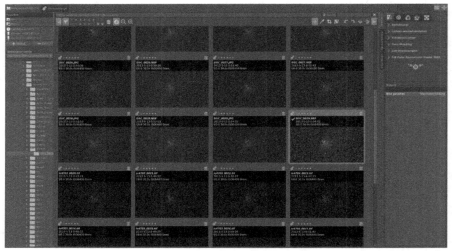

Figure 59: The working screen of RawTherapee. In the left, the file directory, in the middle the thumbnails of images in the selected folder, the manipulation options in the right.

After successful development of all RAW files, use GIMP and/or Fotoxx as described before to create a nice astro photo.

The most important parameters for astrophotography

For an amateur like you and me, light pollution in your neighborhood is the most dominant problem. The parameter **Black** in the exposure register is the tool to fight it. Rising Black lets the background of your image sink into black.

The second important parameter is the **Tone curve** (you have two, 1 and 2, but you can also use just one). The standard type is **Linear**. But when choosing Custom curve, you can adopt the curve to show fine structures as described in the chapter <u>Elaboration of details by changing the gradation curve</u>. The meaning of the tone curves is, to allow using tone curve 1 for lower levels and tone curve 2 for higher levels. This is like using an S-type curve in only one tone curve, but much more detailed.

With these two parameters you will succeed to create useful images for further summing up in GIMP and HDR with Fotoxx. The great advantage of RAW images is the eschewal of information loss by using floating point arithmetic during the development process. But these images also contain the full noise of the image sensor. A part of the noise is reduced by the summing process, which equals some kind of averaging the noise. But you will need a lot of photos (much more than 10) to get meaningful noise reduction. But the noise reduction by averaging does not destroy details in the photo. If you still have annoying noise in the image, use the noise reduction in the GIMP tools.

As a demonstration of how to set the parameters for development, figure 60 shows an example.

The histogram shows the pixel values at the histogram location

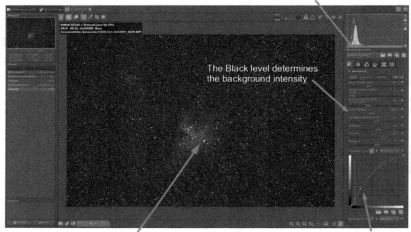

The Black level determines the background intensity

The cursor defines the histogram location

Adapting the tone curve

Figure 60: The development parameters are located in the right part of the window. A mouse click in the image locates the pixel whose values are shown below the histogram. Manipulating the Black parameter allows setting the background intensity. Using the tone curve allows highlighting of faint structures.

Technical Addendum

For those interested in the physics of imaging, I try to give a little overview of what is important to have in mind, when you take your images. There is no guarantee for completeness, but I do my very best to show what is important from my point of view.

Optical paths

Every point of an astronomical object is sending rays of light. Due to the enormous distances in astronomy, we assume the light rays to come to us as a parallel beam of rays. To be seen as a point, the beam has to be manipulated by an optical instrument, either a mirror or a lens, to converge into one point. This point of light causes either a signal on the retina of our eye or on the image sensor's surface. We discuss the main optical tools we have for making photos of astronomical objects.

Refractors (telescopes with lenses)

The kernel of an refractor is the image creating lens. In fact it is not a single lens but a compound of several lenses, designed to be free of optical artefacts. In our presentation of telescope optical paths, we simply assume that an ideal lens is working in the refractor.
This is obviously not the case in reality. The most simple lens is an achromatic lens. It is made up from 2 compound lenses [7]. By the combination of the 2 lenses, the chromatic error for the colours red and blue is corrected. Therefore the name of the lens.
With 3 compound lenses, it is possible to create a lens, which is nearly free of chromatic errors [8]. Obviously such a lens is more complex to manufacture and therefore more expensive. To

distinguish this type of lens from the more simple achromatic lens, it is called an apochromatic lens.

Unfortunately there are more errors coming up with the creation of images like astigmatism, Coma and spherical aberration. The amount of correction is normally directly readable in the price of a lens. Again: In my optical paths all lenses are just drawn as a simple lenses, regardless of the type of construction.

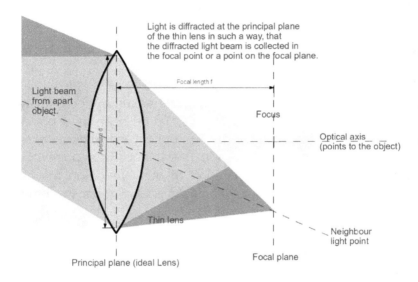

Figure 61: Light from astronomical objects arrives as parallel light beam. The ideal thin lens (represented by the principal plane) refracts the light into the focal point. Neighboured light points touch down in a point of the focal plane, close to the focus.

In figure 61, you can see the optical path of a refractor lens. If the image sensor of a camera is located in the focal plane of the lens, a sharp image results on the image sensor. The distance from the focal point of the lens to the principal plane of the lens is called the focal length of the lens. It is given in millimeter. Another important number is the aperture d. This is the diameter of the lens in

millimeter. The ration $\frac{f}{d}$ is known as aperture ratio, lens aperture or f-stop. This number determines the amount of light getting on to the image sensor. A small f-stop requires less exposure time than a largef-stop, as the amount of light increases with decreasing f-stop. Have a look at your camera's f-stop settings. You will note the following numbers:

Doubling the amount of light

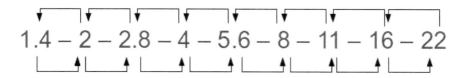

$$1.4 - 2 - 2.8 - 4 - 5.6 - 8 - 11 - 16 - 22$$

Doubling exposure time

For example, a lens with f-stop of 4 will need only half the exposure time of a lens with an f-stop of 5.6, as the amount of light is doubling when the f-stop setting is changed from 5.6 to 4.

Refractor for visual observation

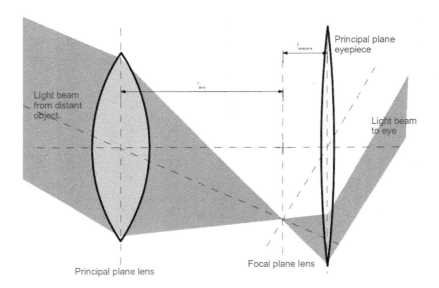

Figure 62: The setup of a Kepler type telescope. The eyepiece works as a magnifying glass, which looks at the focal plane of the lens.

If you want to observe astronomical objects with your eye, the light passing the lens must pass a second lens, the eyepiece. Here the light is refracted again to allow the eye's lens to create a sharp image on the retina. The first man, who described such a telescope consisting of lens and eyepiece was Johannes Kepler. Although Galileo had a few years ago described a telescope, his construction used a concave lens as eyepiece. Keplers construction had better optical properties and therefore was accepted as the standard astronomical refractor telescope (figure 62).

In figure 62, however, the eyepiece and the lens are each represented in a wrong relationship. The eyepiece has a much smaller diameter than the lens. Here the artistic freedom has been stressed to correctly display the light beam passing. The eye sees the incident light beam from the eyepiece as a parallel beam of light from a distant object, just under a larger angle. The image appears to be larger. The magnification V results from the focal lengths of the lens and eyepiece:

$$V = \frac{f_{lens}}{f_{eyepiece}}$$

The Newton reflector telescope

The simplest telescope contains a single imaging concave parabolic mirror (figure 63). However, this design has a drawback: If you want to see the image in the focal plane, you obstruct the incoming light. Isaac Newton found a solution for this problem by putting a small secondary mirror in front of the focal plane, that guides the light out of the path of the incoming light through a hole in the tube of the telescope. So the focal plane is outside the tube (figure 64).

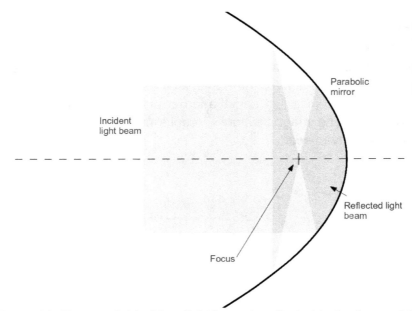

Figure 63: The parallel incident light beam is reflected to the focus of the parabolic mirror.

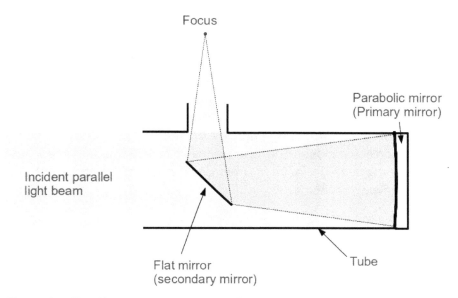

Focus

Parabolic mirror
(Primary mirror)

Incident parallel
light beam

Flat mirror
(secondary mirror)

Tube

Figure 64: The Newtonian telescope reflects the incident parallel light beam by the parabolic (primary) mirror and then uses the flat (secondary) mirror to get the focus out of the tube.

Comparing a refractor type telescope with a newton reflector telescope, it obviously has the advantage of no chromatic error. In addition, newton reflectors can have large apertures [9]. An f-stop of $\frac{f}{d} = 4$ is no problem. Nevertheless focusing such a telescope is a bit critical. A disadvantage is the alignment of the primary and secondary mirrors. This must be controlled frequently.

Other aberrations (mainly coma) are present, but are partly corrected by glass elements (lenses). This is recommendable for newton reflectors of f-stop $\frac{f}{d} = 4$ for two reasons:

1. The coma is reduced.

2. Digital cameras with changeable lenses suffer from dust. Once dust particles land on the image sensors surface, they will forever create dark spots in the image, until the sensor is cleaned. As the newton reflector is an open mechanical system, there is a free pathway from the outside dusty world to the clean room in front of the image sensor. The long exposure times that astronomical photos need, do their contribution to dust particles on the image sensor. A coma corrector closes the open access to the image sensor just like a lens. In fact it is a lens, you put into the focuser of the newton reflector.

The Maksutov-Cassegrain telescope

The Maksutov-Cassegrain telescope also has two mirrors, just like the newton telescope (figure 65). But the primary mirror has a hole in the middle, and the secondary mirror is a concave spherical mirror, carried by a spherical glass plate. The incoming parallel light beam is reflected like in the newton reflector, then reaches the secondary mirror and is reflected through the hole in the primary mirror out of the telescope tube. There the eyepiece or the camera can pick up the light for further use. The chromatic aberration as well as the coma is not visible, so the telescope creates an image of good quality. A further advantage is the compact and lightweight construction, due to the folded light path. A disadvantage is the

reduced f-stop for these telescopes. F-stops of $\frac{f}{d} = 16$ are usual [10].

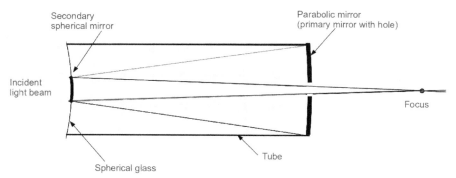

Figure 65: The Maksutov-Cassegrain telescope contains two mirrors and a spherical meniscus lens.

The Schmidt-Cassegrain telescope

This is structured like the Maksutov-Cassegrain telescope. However the front lens is not a simple meniscus like shape but a quite complex formed glass lens to even better correct aberrations [11].

Magnification

One of the most confusing data once you want to buy a telescope is the magnification. There is a maximal magnification for a telescope and a practical magnification, which is smaller than the maximal possible magnification and responsible for the appearance of an object on the sensor of the camera or in your eye. For each of these applications we will see the formulas.

Visual magnification

Definition

The visual magnification is just the relation of the viewing angle of the object with telescope and without telescope (figure 66).

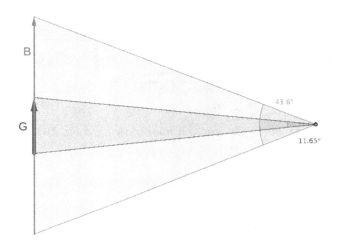

Figure 66: An object G is seen by the angle of 11.6 degrees. Using a telescope, the viewing angle is increased to 43.6 degrees. So the image B seems to be enlarged.

The definition of magnification is:

$$V = \frac{\alpha_B}{\alpha_G}$$

The example in figure 66 then shows a magnification of

$$V = \frac{\alpha_B}{\alpha_G} = \frac{43{,}6\,^\circ}{11{,}65\,^\circ} = 3{,}74$$

How do the data of a Kepler type telescope influence the magnification of a telescope?

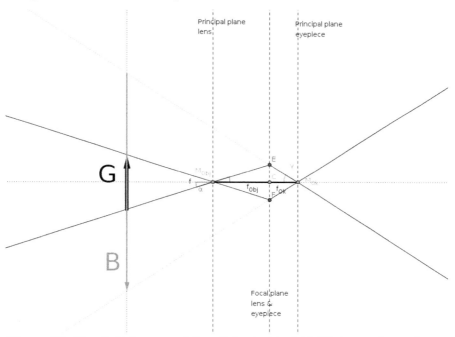

Figure 67: The light beams of the distant object G (Galaxy, star, …) pass through the midpoint of the lens and create an image in the focal plane of the lens, which is also the focal plane of the eyepiece. The eyepiece refracts the light beams so, as if they originated from the focal plane.

Figure 67 shows how the image B of the object G is formed with the formed with the help of lens and eyepiece. See also figure 62. You can see from figure 67, that the tangent of the lens angle and the tangent of the eyepiece angle are as large as the angles themselves, once the object is far away and therefore the angles are small. Using the definition of magnification this gives:

$$V = \frac{\gamma}{\alpha} \approx \frac{tan(\gamma)}{tan(\alpha)} = \frac{\frac{\overline{EC}}{f_{eyepiece}}}{\frac{\overline{EC}}{f_{lens}}} = \frac{f_{lens}}{f_{eyepiece}}$$

The visual magnification of the telescope with objective and eyepiece is equal to the ratio of focal length of the lens to the focal length of the eyepiece. The larger the focal length for the same eyepiece, the greater the magnification. Conversely, the smaller the eyepiece focal length with the same focal length of the lens, the greater the magnification. Maximum magnification is thus obtained with a large focal length and a small eyepiece focal length. The wave theory of light is limiting the magnification to a maximum magnification. In practice, this rule of thumb limits the practical magnification:

$$V_{max} = 2 * aperture$$

where the aperture of the lens is measured in millimeters [12] .

Photographic magnification

Unlike the visual magnification, in photography we only have one lens and no eyepiece. So there is no relation of focus lengths. We have to come back to the basic definition of magnification: The relation of the viewing angle without lens (naked eye) and the viewing angle with a (telephoto)lens.

In photography, a focal length with the size of the diagonal of the image sensor has been adopted as normal [13]. But in practice, for cameras using the 24mmx36mm format (the original 35mm film format) a focal length of f=50mm has been adopted as normal. For the magnification of a lens, we have to compare the viewing angle of a tele lens with that of a normal lens with f=50mm, once we are talking about 35mm film cameras.

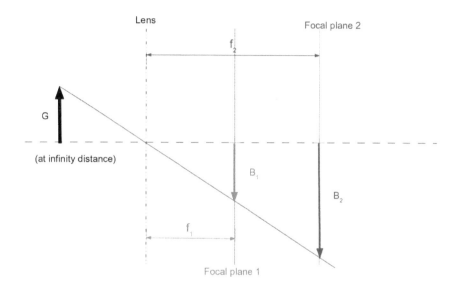

Figure 68: The image of an object at infinite distance is created in the focal plane of a lens. A lens with small focal length (f1) creates the image closer to the lens. The image B1 is therefore smaller than that (B2) of a lens with large focal length f2. The relation of the size of the two images gives the photographic magnification.

A camera with a tele lens of $f_2 = 100mm$ creates an image, which is larger than the image created with the normal lens of $f_1 = 50mm$. Figure 68 gives a magnification of 2:

$$V = \frac{B_2}{B1} = \frac{f_2}{f_1} = \frac{100mm}{50mm} = 2$$

Magnification using afocal eye piece projection

Using afocal eye piece projection, the image on the sensor is created by the camera lens, just like it is by the humans eye lens. This means, that the optical path is determined by three lenses: The objective lens, the eye piece lens and the camera lens (figure 69).

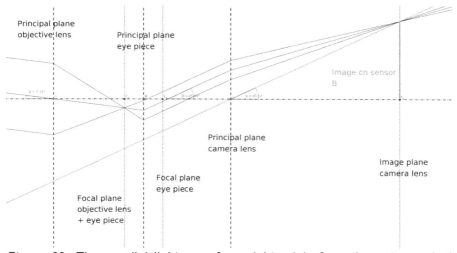

Figure 69: The parallel light rays from right origin from the astronomical object. The objective lens creates an image in the common focal plane of the objective and the eye piece. The eye piece lens creates a parallel bundle of light, which is taken by the camera lens, which creates the image on the sensor.

This complex setup allows to manipulate the magnification at three locations:

- Focal length of **objective lens**: The larger the focal length, the greater the image in the focal plane of the objective lens.
- Focal length of the **eye piece lens**: The smaller the focal length of the eye piece lens, the larger the viewing angle, under which the image is seen.
- Focal length of the **camera lens**: The larger the focus length of the camera lens, the larger the image on the sensor.

As it is a photographic image, we have to use the equation for photographic magnification. But instead of using the focal length of the objective lens, he eye piece lens or the camera lens, we have to use the effective lens, calculated according to:

$$\tan(\alpha) = \frac{B}{f_{\;eff}} \Leftrightarrow B = f_{\;eff} * \tan(\alpha)$$

$$\tan(\gamma) = \frac{B}{f_{\;camera}} \Leftrightarrow B = f_{\;camera} * \tan(\gamma)$$

$$\Rightarrow f_{\;eff} * \tan(\alpha) = f_{\;camera} * \tan(\gamma) \Leftrightarrow f_{\;eff} = f_{\;camera} * \frac{\tan(\gamma)}{\tan(\alpha)} = f_{\;camera} * V$$

$$\Rightarrow f_{\;eff} = \frac{f_{\;camera} * f_{\;objective}}{f_{\;eye\;piece}}$$

These three focal lengths allow easily to reach large effective focal length, easily exceeding the <u>useful magnification</u>, determined by the diameter of the objective lens.

Magnification using focal eye piece projection

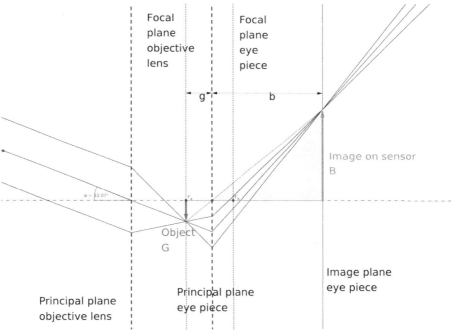

Figure 70: Using focal eye piece projection, the image on the sensor is created by the eye piece lens.

We use the same equation for the calculation of the magnification as with the afocal eye piece projection:

$$f_{\mathit{eff}} = \frac{B}{\tan(\alpha)}$$

As the eye piece lens works like the lens of a diascope, we can use the general lens equation:

$$\frac{1}{b} + \frac{1}{g} = \frac{1}{f_{eye\ piece}}$$

$$\Leftrightarrow 1 + \frac{b}{g} = \frac{b}{f_{eye\ piece}}$$

$$\Leftrightarrow \frac{b}{g} = \frac{b - f_{eye\ piece}}{f_{eye\ piece}}$$

Furthermore we take from figure 70 due to the intercept theorem of mathematics:

$$\frac{B}{G} = \frac{b}{g}$$

For the image the objective lens creates (which is the object of the eye piece lens), we have:

$$f_{objective} = \frac{G}{tan(\alpha)} \Leftrightarrow tan(\alpha) = \frac{G}{f_{objective}}$$

Inserting this value of tan(α) into the equation for the effective focal length, you receive:

$$f_{eff} = \frac{B}{G} * f_{objective} = \frac{b}{g} * f_{objective} = \frac{b - f_{eye\ piece}}{f_{eye\ piece}} * f_{objective}$$

$$f_{eff} = \frac{f_{objective}}{f_{eye\ piece}} * (b - f_{eye\ piece})$$

The effective focal length is like that of the afocal eye piece projection an easy target for exceeding the useful magnification.

Size of image sensor and magnification

Once you have an image sensor in the 35mm dimension (24mmx36mm, full format sensor), you can simply adopt the calculation above. The magnification V is:

$$V = \frac{f_{telescope}}{50mm}$$

Unfortunately, with the advent of digital photography, the good old 35mm format has lost its meaning, mainly for two reasons:

1. It is very expensive to manufacture large image sensors. The larger the image sensor, the higher the probability of a defect pixel. That's the reason, why cheap consumer cameras use very small image sensors.
2. The smaller the image sensor, the smaller the normal focal length. A short focal length on the other hand, means a compact camera.

Todays digital cameras most probably have one of the sensors of table 5 built in.

Name	1/ 2.3"	2/3"	FourThirds	Foveon	APS-C (Canon)	Full format (35mm)
Dimension [mm]	6.2x4.6	8.8x6.6	17.3x13.0	20.7x13.8	22.2x14.8	24x36
Diagonal length [mm]	7.7	11.0	21.3	24.9	27.1	43.3
Crop factor (magnification vs. 35mm format)	5.6	4.0	2.0	1.7	1.6	1.0
Application	Compact cameras without changeable lens.	High level compact cameras without changeable lens.	DSLR and mirrorless system cameras (FT and MFT bayonet).	DSLR with interchangeable lenses. The sensor has a different structure than usual.	DSLR with interchangeable lenses.	High valued DSLR or classical 35mm film cameras.

Table 5: Dimensions of image sensors in digital cameras ([14], [15], State of 2012).

The diagonal length in table 5 also shows the focal length of the normal lens. As already written, the 35mm normal lens should be f=43.3mm, but for practical reasons has been changed to f=50mm. For the calculation of the crop factor, the real diagonal size has been taken as the column of the diagonal length shows. In order to calculate the magnification, you can bring in the crop factor into the last equation, giving:

$$V = \frac{b * f}{50\text{mm}}$$

Here b is the crop factor from table 5, all other variables are known.

Field of view (FOV)

Looking through a telescope, the field of view is also an interesting quantity.

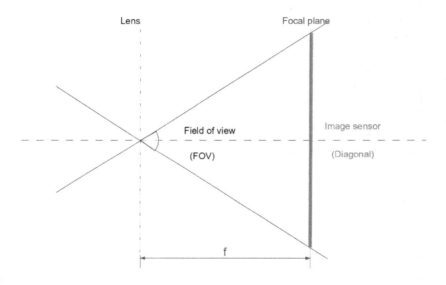

Figure 71: The field of view results from the diagonal length of the image sensor.

According to figure 71, the field of view α is calculated by

$$\alpha = 2 * \arctan\left(\frac{\frac{d}{2}}{\frac{f}{2}}\right) = 2 * \arctan\left(\frac{d}{f}\right)$$

Herein d is the diagonal length of the image sensor from table 5 and f the focal length of the lens (telescope). You do not need to have a crop factor in mind. This is already contained in the diagonal length. You can use this FOV in Kstars and Stellarium to plan the use of the telescope for a certain object. Once you zoom in or out, the FOV is shown either in the low left corner (Kstars) or in the middle of the status line at the bottom window frame (Stellarium). Table 6 shows the combinations for my equipment.

Telescope f [mm]	FOV [°]		
	APS-C	FourThirds Micro FourThirds	Full size (35mm)
400	7,8	6,1	12,4
714	4,3	3,4	6,9
800	3,9	3,1	6,2
1250	2,5	2,0	4,0

Table 6: FOV for my telescopes and cameras.

Once you have NGC7000 on your target list, Stellarium shows a FOV of 2° for that object. As you need some space around the object, a telescope with a focal length of f=400mm using the FT/MFT or APS-C camera seems useful. A full format (35mm) sensor would need f=800mm or f=714mm instead.

Once you use table 6 to set your FOV in Kstars or Stellarium, you will see the sky as you get it on your image sensor.

Sources and links

1. http://en.wikipedia.org/wiki/Messier_object
2. https://fotoalbum.gmx.net/ui/external/_W9dkqzRTEC8I02-HsNGVA84801
3. Klaus Gölker: GIMP 2 for Photographers: Image Editing with Open Source Software, ISBN-13: 978-1-93395-203-1
4. http://www.gimp.org/
5. http://edu.kde.org/kstars/
6. http://www.stellarium.org/
7. http://upload.wikimedia.org/wikipedia/commons/thumb/1/15/Lens6b-en.svg/2000px-Lens6b-en.svg.png
8. http://upload.wikimedia.org/wikipedia/commons/thumb/9/91/Apochromat.svg/2000px-Apochromat.svg.png
9. http://en.wikipedia.org/wiki/Newtonian_telescope
10. http://en.wikipedia.org/wiki/Maksutov_telescope
11. http://en.wikipedia.org/wiki/Schmidt%E2%80%93Cassegrain_telescope
12. http://www.nexstarsite.com/_RAC/articles/formulas.htm
13. http://en.wikipedia.org/wiki/Normal_lens
14. http://en.wikipedia.org/wiki/Crop_factor
15. http://en.wikipedia.org/wiki/Image_sensor_format
16. http://www.kornelix.com/fotoxx.html
17. http://rawtherapee.com/
18. http://sourceforge.net/projects/indi/
19. http://gphoto.sourceforge.net/
20. http://www.darktable.org/

www.ingramcontent.com/pod-product-compliance
Lightning Source LLC
LaVergne TN
LVHW052124070326
832902LV00038B/3645